the
SUGAR-
FREE
recipe book

the SUGAR-FREE

recipe book

Over 70 delicious recipes to help shed weight safely

Bounty
Books

An Hachette UK Company
www.hachette.co.uk

First published in Great Britain in 2014 by Bounty Books,
a division of Octopus Publishing Group Ltd
Carmelite House, 50 Victoria Embankment, London EC4Y 0DZ
www.octopusbooks.co.uk

ISBN: 978-0-7537-2836-9

A CIP catalogue record for this book is available from the British Library

Printed and bound in China

10 9 8 7 6 5 4 3

Disclaimer/Publisher's note

Publisher: Samantha Warrington
Editorial and Design Manager: Emma Hill
Editor: Jane Birch
Designer: Chris Bell/cbdesign
Production Controller: Caroline Alberti

contents

introduction   6

snacks & savoury bakes   12

soups & salads   30

lunches & light meals   58

family favourites   76

food for friends   102

index   126

acknowledgements   128

introduction

all about sugar

The Western world is facing an epidemic of obesity and, with it, Type 2 diabetes and heart disease. We are getting fatter and fatter, despite the fact that people are exercising more than ever. Today, 26 per cent of Britons are obese and half the population is overweight. In the United States, around one in three adults is obese.

For years, the fight against increasing weight levels and related health issues, such as heart disease, has targeted fat as the enemy. This dates back to the late 1950s and American Dr Ancel Keys's Seven Countries Study, which looked at rates of heart disease and diet in 22 countries and linked a diet high in fat with a corresponding high rate of heart disease. But Keys cherry-picked his data, choosing results from only seven countries, omitting places like France and West Germany, which had low rates of heart disease despite the high fat content of their diet.

Sugar fact
We consume an average of 140 spoons of sugar per week.

Now diet advice is shifting as new research points the finger firmly, not at fat, but at sugar, specifically the huge amount of it we consume. And it is a huge amount: British people consume on average more than 500g (1 lb) of sugar a week.

sugar is addictive

'Chocaholic, 'craving a biscuit', 'a bit of a cake junkie' – we bandy phrases like this about casually, but there is evidence to show that sugar addiction is real. Among the studies to support this is the 2007 research by scientists in Bordeaux, France, that showed that in animal trials, rats chose sugar over cocaine, even when they were addicted to cocaine.

fructose

The reason sugar is so bad for us is that it is half glucose, half fructose. Glucose is a good guy: it is vital for health and can be metabolized by most cells in the body.

Fructose, on the other hand, is a real problem. The only organ that can process fructose is the liver and most of it gets converted directly to fat. And when you consume fructose in liquid form, in fruit juice or fizzy drinks, this happens even faster.

Sugar fact
Fructose converts directly to fat in the body.

The other problem is how much we eat of it. Hormones is our body tell us when we've had enough protein, fat or carbohydrate. There is one carbohydrate that is the exception to this – fructose. Some scientists think that fructose fools our body into thinking we're not full so we keep eating it. In other words, there is no 'off' switch for fructose.

Eating all that sugar makes us fatter and less healthy. In addition, the more we eat, the more blood sugar levels rise until we can't produce enough insulin to get rid of the blood sugar. This is what is known as insulin resistance, which can be a precursor to Type 2 diabetes.

No wonder then that governments and health experts the world over are increasingly concerned and that the World Health Organization has recommended that we should halve the daily amount of sugar we eat.

what going sugar free can do for you

Eating excess sugar has been associated with obesity, diabetes and heart disease, so cutting right back on sugar has obvious health benefits. But there are other benefits too. Going sugar free can also lead to weight loss, more energy, better skin, less bloating and looking younger.

In fact, scientists from Leiden University in the Netherlands have established a clear link between the amount of sugar in the blood and how old a person looks. They measured the blood sugar levels of men and women aged between 50 and 70, asked an independent panel to assess their ages from photographs and found that those with high blood sugar looked significantly older.

secret sugar

It is easy to pinpoint and cut out the obvious sources of sugar – sweets, biscuits, cakes, desserts and so on – but what about the secret sugar?

Cooking sauces, condiments, cereals, bread, crackers, coleslaw, flavoured cottage cheese, dips, processed meats, tinned tomatoes, bottled salad dressings… There is hidden sugar lurking in all sorts of your store cupboard standbys and not just where you'd expect to find it, in fizzy drinks and doughnuts. For instance, there are as many as 5 teaspoons of sugar per can in some brands of baked beans and bread can contain up to ½ a teaspoon of sugar per slice. Bottled pasta sauce can have up to 6 teaspoons of added sugar while balsamic vinegar has 15 times more sugar than cider vinegar.

Perhaps surprisingly, low-fat and 'healthy' brands are among the worst for added sugar. That's because, to add flavour, the fat is replaced with sugar. Think about the 12 g of sugar (around 3 teaspoons) that may be in that granola bar next time you reach for one. Another one to consider is yogurt: full-fat natural yogurt has around a third of the sugar of low-fat natural yogurt.

Even those foods marked 'no added sugar' can have fructose added in other forms, such as fruit juice and agave syrup.

The only way to be sure about hidden sugar, which can vary dramatically from product to product, is to check the label before you buy. Sugars are listed as a sub-category under carbohydrates.

Tip
Always check the nutritional information on packaging for the sugar content before you buy.

how much sugar?

Opinions differ on this. The National Health Service in the UK recommends no more than 10 teaspoons (40 g) per day, while the World Health Organization suggests a limit of 6 teaspoons. The American Heart Association guidelines are no more that 6 teaspoons a day for women and 9 teaspoons for men.

To work out how many spoons of sugar something contains, divide the grams by 4. This is roughly equal to 1 teaspoon.

fructose in fruit

Everyone knows fruit, which is delicious plus being packed with nutrients and fibre, is good for you but what about the fructose in it? If you are cutting down on other sources of fructose, then it is fine to enjoy a couple of small pieces of fruit a day. From a fructose point of view, there are some things to consider: very sweet fruit tends to have a higher fructose content. Grapes, watermelon and bananas (at around 7 teaspoons of sugar per banana), for instance, are very high fructose, while berries, citrus (especially grapefruit), plums and kiwifruit are relatively low.

Tip
Aim to keep your fruit intake to two small pieces of fruit per day and up your daily veg intake.

When it comes to fruit, however, there are two big no-nos: fruit juice and dried fruit. A medium 250 ml (8 fl oz) glass of cranberry juice contains a massive 36 g of sugar. A glass of apple juice, no matter how freshly squeezed, contains the same amount of sugar as a glass of non-diet cola: around 8 teaspoons!

Dried fruit should be avoided too, even the fruit we think of as savoury, such as sun-dried tomatoes (this goes for sun-dried tomato paste, too). Drying fruit concentrates the sugars as the same time as losing the bulk that will make you feel full.

sugar swaps

Here are some of the key culprits and some low-sugar alternatives:

Sugar suspects	Try this instead
balsamic vinegar	cider vinegar, wine vinegar
many condiments, especially tomato ketchup & barbecue sauce	mustard, Tabasco
sweet chilli sauce	tamari
low-fat mayonnaise	full-fat mayonnaise
low-fat yogurt	full-fat yogurt
salad cream	full-fat mayonnaise
white and wholemeal bread	rye bread, sourdough bread
jam, marmalade etc	yeast spread, cream cheese, unsweetened peanut butter
curry paste, especially Thai	ground curry spices
chutney and relishes	fresh homemade salsas
bottled pasta sauces	homemade sauces and passata
soft drinks, mixers and fruit squash	diet versions

Sugar fact
Don't be fooled by so-called 'healthy' sweeteners. Agave syrup is a whopping 90% fructose, while maple syrup and honey are both around 40% fructose.

refined carbs

Any food with a high glycaemic index (GI) will cause a spike in blood glucose. Obviously, sugar and foods containing sugar come into this category and are to be avoided. You should also aim to cut down on processed 'white' carbs, like pasta, rice, couscous and white bread, and go for lower-GI options like rye bread, brown rice, bulghur wheat and so on.

good things to eat

There is growing evidence that the Mediterranean diet, rich in fish, nuts, vegetables and olive oil, could be our healthiest choice. Take the sugar out of your diet and add in some of these ingredients, for an extra health boost. Together with vegetables – aim to 'eat the rainbow' by having a wide range of colours and varieties daily – these are all health-giving superfoods:

- avocados
- eggs
- nuts & seeds
- quinoa & other grains
- oily fish
- lentils & pulses

easy does it

Remember, too, not to get carried away with compensating for cutting out sugar by over-indulging in other foods. Things that you once thought of as 'naughty', such as full-fat cheese, cream and bacon, are all fine for a sugar-free diet but don't overdo it.

Learning portion control is key to a healthy lifestyle and a slim waistline, whatever diet you follow. And, when it comes to second helpings, try to wait 20 minutes to see if you really are hungry.

treat yourself

Obviously cakes, biscuits, sweets, puddings and the like are out, but you won't feel deprived as there are still plenty of delicious treats. Aim to replace your after-dinner chocolate ice cream, for instance, with a couple of oatcakes and a small piece of really special cheese (don't forget to skip the chutney, though). Instead of a bag of sweets, have a bowl of popcorn or a small bag of potato crisps. As always, read the nutrition label – for instance, crisps with additional flavourings such as Thai sweet chilli or Worcestershire sauce tend to contain significantly more sugar.

And, the good news is, you can still enjoy a glass of wine or beer. The drier the wine, the better so pass on the fortified or dessert wines. Pure spirits are fine too but watch the mixers. Tonic water, for instance, is very high in sugar so always opt for a diet version. As always, when it comes to alcohol, moderation is the key.

What about chocolate?
This really should be avoided but, if you absolutely must, have a square or two of the highest cocoa content. Just remember that anything in that bar that isn't cocoa is sugar.

snacks &
savoury bakes

smoked mackerel crostini

serves 4
prep + cook time 12–13 minutes

230 g (7½ oz) smoked mackerel
   fillets, skinned
1 tablespoon creamed horseradish
2 tablespoons crème fraîche
1 tablespoon chopped chives
finely grated rind of 1 lemon
1 tablespoon lemon juice
1 granary or seeded baguette,
   sliced
1 spring onion, finely sliced
   diagonally (optional)
2 little gem lettuces, leaves
   separated
pepper

1 Put the smoked mackerel in a bowl and break into flakes with a fork. Add the horseradish, crème fraîche, chives, lemon rind and juice and plenty of pepper and mix together gently.
2 Place the sliced baguette on a grill pan and cook under a preheated medium-hot grill for 2–3 minutes or until crisp and golden, turning once. Serve the hot crostini immediately with the smoked mackerel paté, spring onion, if liked, and the lettuce leaves.

Tip
Horseradish is a perfect complement to smoked mackerel and roast beef. It contains some sugar, so always use sparingly and look for the brand lowest in sugar.

butter bean & anchovy pâté

serves 2–3
prep time 5 minutes

425 g (14 oz) can butter beans,
    drained and rinsed
50 g (2 oz) can anchovy fillets in oil
2 spring onions, finely chopped
2 tablespoons lemon juice
1 tablespoon olive oil
4 tablespoons chopped coriander
salt and pepper
lemon wedges
4–6 slices rye bread, toasted

1 Put all the ingredients except the coriander in a food processor or blender and process until well mixed but not smooth. Alternatively, mash the beans with a fork, finely chop the anchovies and mix the ingredients together by hand.
2 Stir in the coriander and season well. Serve with lemon wedges and accompanied with toasted rye bread.

Tip
Rye bread is low GI, wheat free and has up to four times the fibre of standard white bread.

broad bean & mint hummus
with wholegrain crostini

serves 4
prep time 10 minutes

250 g (8 oz) frozen peas
250 g (8 oz) frozen baby broad
   beans, preferably peeled
1 wholegrain or granary baguette,
   sliced
125 g (4 oz) Greek yogurt
2 tablespoons lemon juice
2 tablespoons chopped mint
salt and pepper
toasted sesame seeds, to garnish

1 Put the peas and beans in a bowl and pour over enough boiling water to cover completely. Cover with a plate and set aside for 3 minutes. Drain and quickly cool under running cold water.

2 Meanwhile, place the slices of baguette under a preheated grill to toast for 1–2 minutes each side until golden brown.

3 Place the peas and beans in a food processor or blender. Add the yogurt, lemon juice and 1 tablespoon of the mint and blend until almost smooth. Scrape into a bowl and stir through the remaining mint, then season with salt and pepper.

4 Spoon the pea and mint hummus into small bowls, scatter over toasted sesame seeds and serve with the toasted baguette slices.

tapas

roasted almonds with paprika

serves 6   **prep + cook time** 22 minutes

300 g (10 oz) blanched almonds
2 teaspoons olive oil
1 teaspoon sweet smoked paprika
1½ teaspoons sea salt flakes

1 Place the almonds on a baking sheet and roast in a preheated oven, 180°C (350°F), Gas Mark 4, for 15 minutes until starting to brown.
2 Stir through the remaining ingredients, return to the oven and cook for a further 2 minutes until heated through. Leave to cool, then serve.

haloumi with paprika oil

serves 4   **prep + cook time** 10 minutes

6 tablespoons extra virgin olive oil
4 tablespoons lemon juice
½ teaspoon smoked paprika
250 g (8 oz) haloumi cheese, cut into chunks
salt and pepper

1 Combine the oil, lemon juice and paprika in a small bowl and season the mixture with salt and pepper.
2 Heat a heavy-based frying pan until hot, then add the haloumi and toss over a medium heat until golden and starting to soften. Transfer immediately to a plate, drizzle over the paprika oil and serve with cocktail sticks to spike the haloumi.

baked chillies with cheese

serves 6   **prep + cook time** 25–30 minutes

175 g (6 oz) cream cheese
100 g (3½ oz) goats' cheese
100 g (3½ oz) Cheddar cheese, grated
2 spring onions, sliced
12 fresh jalapeño chillies, deseeded, if liked, and halved
1 tomato, chopped

1 Place the cheeses in a bowl and mix together until smooth, then gently stir in the spring onions. Spoon a little of the cheese mixture into each chilli half, filling the cavity.
2 Transfer the chillies to a lightly oiled baking sheet and scatter over the tomato. Bake in a preheated oven, 200°C (400°F), Gas Mark 6, for 10–15 minutes until soft and lightly charred.

citrus olives

serves 6   **prep + cook time** 6 minutes + marinating overnight (optional)

2 teaspoons fennel seeds
finely grated rind and juice of ½ lemon
finely grated rind and juice of ¼ orange
75 ml (3 fl oz) olive oil
400 g (13 oz) mixed olives

1 Place the fennel seeds in a small, dry frying pan and toast for 30 seconds until they start to pop and emit an aroma. Remove from the pan and roughly crush.
2 Mix together the fennel seeds, grated rind and juice and oil in a non-metallic bowl, then stir in the olives. Serve immediately or cover and leave to marinate overnight in a cool place before serving.

guacamole with vegetable dippers

serves 4
prep time 10 minutes

2 large, ripe avocados
½ small red onion
2 tablespoons lime juice
3 tablespoons finely chopped
  coriander
¼ teaspoon garlic powder
¼ teaspoon celery salt
pinch of cayenne
½ teaspoon paprika
3 tomatoes
few dashes of Tabasco (optional)
salt and pepper

to serve
350 g (11½ oz) carrots, cut into
  batons
350 g (11½ oz) cauliflower florets
4 celery sticks, cut into batons
250 g (8 oz) radishes, trimmed
125 g (4 oz) baby sweetcorn

1 Peel the avocados and remove the stones, then mash the flesh in a small bowl with the back of a fork or potato masher to break it up.
2 Finely chop the red onion and add to the avocado along with the lime juice, coriander, garlic powder, celery salt and spices. Mix until almost smooth, with some small lumps, then season with salt and pepper.
3 Quarter, deseed and finely chop the tomatoes, then stir them into the avocado mixture. Add the Tabasco, if using.
4 Scoop into a serving bowl and arrange on a platter with the selection of raw vegetables.

Tip
Unlike many condiments, Tabasco is a great choice for a sugar-free lifestyle. Try adding to soups and stews for a little extra kick.

parsnip & beetroot crisps with dukkah

serves 4
prep + cook time 30 minutes

sunflower or vegetable oil,
   for deep-frying
2 parsnips, peeled, halved and
   thinly sliced lengthways
2–3 raw beetroot, peeled and
   thinly sliced
salt and pepper

spice mix
1 tablespoon hazelnuts
1 tablespoon sesame seeds
2 teaspoons cumin seeds
2 teaspoons coriander seeds
2 teaspoons dried mint

1 To make the spice mix, dry-fry the hazelnuts and seeds in a small, heavy-based frying pan over a medium heat for 2–3 minutes until they emit a nutty aroma. Using a pestle and mortar, pound the nuts and seeds to a coarse powder, or tip into a spice grinder and grind to a fine powder. Stir in the mint and season well. Set aside.

2 In a deep saucepan, heat enough oil for deep-frying to 180–190°C (350–375°F), or until a cube of bread browns in 30 seconds. Deep-fry the parsnips in batches until lightly golden. Remove with a slotted spoon and drain on kitchen paper, then tip all the parsnips into a bowl while hot and sprinkle over half the dukkah spice mix.

3 Reduce the heat (the beetroot slices burn easily) and deep-fry the beetroot in batches. Remove and drain as above, then tip into a bowl and sprinkle with the remaining spice mix. Serve the parsnip and beetroot crisps separately, or mixed together.

Tip
Homemade vegetable crisps are not only a delicious treat, but you can be absolutely certain they have no added sugar.

root chips with parsley mayonnaise

serves 4
prep + cook time 40–45 minutes

2 sweet potatoes, cut into slim
  wedges with skin on
1 large baking potato, cut into slim
  wedges with skin on
2 parsnips, cut into long wedges
3 tablespoons olive oil
1 teaspoon Cajun seasoning
3 tablespoons chopped parsley

parsley mayonnaise
1 egg
150 ml (¼ pint) olive oil
½ teaspoon mustard powder
1 tablespoon white wine vinegar
1 tablespoon chopped parsley

1 Put the sweet potato, baking potato and parsnip wedges in a bowl and drizzle with the olive oil, tossing well to coat lightly. Sprinkle with the Cajun seasoning and toss again to coat. Transfer to a large baking sheet and roast in a preheated oven, 200°C (400°F), Gas Mark 6, for 25–30 minutes, until the vegetables are crisp and golden.
2 Meanwhile, make the mayonnaise. Place all the ingredients except the parsley in a small measuring jug, and using an electric blender whiz until a thick mayonnaise is formed. Stir in the parsley.
3 Serve the chips tossed with the parsley, with a bowl of the mayonnaise, for dipping.

For cheese & chive mayonnaise, make the mayonnaise as above and stir in 2 tablespoons soured cream, 1 tablespoon freshly grated Parmesan cheese and 2 tablespoons fresh snipped chives.

rosemary, bacon & brie muffins

makes 8
prep + cook time 30 minutes

75 g (3 oz) rindless streaky bacon
    rashers, finely chopped
225 g (7½ oz) plain flour
1½ teaspoons baking powder
1 teaspoon bicarbonate of soda
1 teaspoon sweet paprika
2 large eggs
¼ teaspoon black pepper
pinch of salt
2 teaspoons finely chopped
    rosemary
150 ml (¼ pint) milk
75 g (3 oz) butter, melted
125 g (4 oz) firm Brie cheese,
    cut into cubes

1 Cook the bacon in a large frying pan over a high heat for 3–4 minutes, stirring occasionally, until golden. Drain on kitchen paper.

2 Meanwhile, sift the flour into a large bowl with the baking powder, bicarbonate of soda and paprika.

3 Break the eggs into a jug and beat lightly. Add the pepper, salt, rosemary, milk and melted butter and whisk together. Pour the mixture into the dry ingredients, add ⅔ of both the Brie and cooked bacon and stir until barely combined.

4 Butter a 12-hole muffin tin. Divide the mixture between the prepared holes, top with the remaining bacon and Brie and bake in a preheated oven, 200°C (400°F), Gas Mark 6, for 18–22 minutes, until risen and golden. Serve warm.

corn & bacon muffins

makes 12
prep + cook time 30–35 minutes

6 streaky bacon rashers, excess
   fat removed, finely chopped
1 small red onion, finely chopped
200 g (7 oz) frozen sweetcorn
175 g (6 oz) fine cornmeal
125 g (4 oz) plain flour
2 teaspoons baking powder
50 g (2 oz) Cheddar cheese, grated
200 ml (7 fl oz) milk
2 eggs
3 tablespoons vegetable oil

1 Lightly oil a 12-hole muffin tin.
2 Dry-fry the bacon and onion in a nonstick frying pan over a medium heat for 3–4 minutes until the bacon is turning crisp. Meanwhile, cook the sweetcorn in a saucepan of boiling water for 2 minutes to soften. Drain.
3 Put the cornmeal, flour and baking powder in a bowl and mix together. Add the sweetcorn, cheese, bacon and onions, then stir in.
4 Whisk the milk with the eggs and oil in a separate bowl, then add to the dry ingredients. Stir gently until just combined, then divide the mixture between the prepared holes.
5 Bake in a preheated oven, 220°C (425°F), Gas Mark 7, for 15–20 minutes until golden and just firm. Loosen the edges of the muffins with a knife and transfer to a wire rack to cool.

For spiced corn & spring onion muffins, omit the bacon and replace the red onion with 4 thinly sliced spring onions. Add 1 teaspoon hot paprika and 1 deseeded and finely chopped red chilli to the mixture before baking as above.

wholemeal cheese straws

makes 12–16
prep + cook time 20 minutes

100 g (3½ oz) wholemeal plain
    flour, plus extra for dusting
2 teaspoons paprika
150 g (5 oz) mature Cheddar
    cheese, grated
100 g (3½ oz) chilled unsalted
    butter, diced
2 teaspoons baking powder
2 egg yolks

1 Mix together the flour and paprika in a bowl, then stir in the cheese. Add the butter and rub in with the fingertips until the mixture resembles fine breadcrumbs. Stir in the baking powder, then add the egg yolks and mix to a stiff dough.

2 Turn the dough out on to a floured surface and press or roll out to about 5 mm (¼ inch) thick. Cut into 1 cm (½ inch) wide straws and place on a baking sheet.

3 Bake in a preheated oven, 220°C (425°F), Gas Mark 7, for 10–12 minutes until golden. Transfer to a wire rack to cool.

herbed soda breads

makes 8
prep + cook time 35–40 minutes

250 g (8 oz) wholemeal flour,
    plus extra for dusting
250 g (8 oz) plain flour
1 teaspoon bicarbonate of soda
1 teaspoon salt
50 g (2 oz) butter, chilled and
    diced, plus extra for greasing
1 spring onion, finely chopped
1 tablespoon chopped parsley
1 tablespoon chopped thyme
1 tablespoon chopped rosemary
275 ml (9 fl oz) buttermilk, or
    ordinary milk soured with
    1 tablespoon lemon juice

1 Sift the flours, bicarbonate of soda and salt into a bowl. Add the butter and rub in with your fingertips until the mixture resembles fine breadcrumbs. Add the spring onion and the herbs and mix well to combine. Make a well in the centre and add the buttermilk or soured milk. Mix with a round-bladed knife to make a soft dough. Turn out on to a lightly floured work surface and knead lightly into a ball. Divide the dough between 8 greased dariole moulds.

2 Place the dariole moulds on a baking sheet, flatten the dough slightly and dust with flour.

3 Bake in a preheated oven, 220°C (425°F), Gas Mark 7, for about 25–30 minutes until risen, golden and hollow sounding when tapped underneath. Transfer to a wire rack to cool. For a softer crust, wrap the hot breads in a clean tea towel to cool. Eat on the day they are made.

rosemary oatcakes

makes 20–24
prep + cook time 30 minutes

200 g (7 oz) rolled oats
3 rosemary sprigs, leaves stripped
125 g (4 oz) plain flour, plus extra
   for dusting
¾ teaspoon baking powder
pinch of salt
75 g (3 oz) chilled unsalted butter,
   diced
100 ml (3½ fl oz) milk

1 Place the oats and rosemary in a food processor and process until they resemble breadcrumbs. Add the flour, baking powder and salt and blitz again. Add the butter, then process until it is mixed in. With the motor still running, pour in the milk through the feed tube until the dough forms a ball.

2 Turn the dough out on to a floured surface and roll out to about 4–5 mm (¼ inch) thick. Cut out 20–24 rounds using a 5–6 cm (2–2½ inch) plain biscuit cutter, re-rolling the trimmings as necessary.

3 Place on a baking sheet and bake in a preheated oven, 190°C (375°F), Gas Mark 5, for 12–15 minutes until golden at the edges. Transfer to a wire rack to cool. Store in an airtight container.

Tip
These sugar-free oatcakes, with a delicate hint of rosemary, are especially delicious with soft and blue cheeses.

soups & salads

chilled avocado soup

serves 4
prep time 20 minutes

4 large, ripe avocados, peeled
    and stoned
juice of 1 lime
½ red chilli, deseeded and diced
900 ml (1½ pints) vegetable stock,
    chilled
2 spring onions, finely sliced
½ red pepper, deseeded and diced
¼ cucumber, diced
1 tablespoon coriander leaves
2 tablespoons olive oil
2 teaspoons lemon juice
2 tablespoons pumpkin seeds,
    toasted
salt and pepper
8 ice cubes, to serve

1 Place the avocados, lime juice and chilli in a food processor and blend with the chilled stock until smooth. Season to taste with salt and pepper and chill for 15 minutes.
2 Meanwhile, mix together the remaining ingredients.
3 Place 2 ice cubes in each of 4 shallow bowls, and pour over the soup.
4 Sprinkle over the salsa and serve.

Tip
Made with health-boosting avocado, this refreshing soup is a great choice for a summer lunch. Sunflower seeds, rich in B complex vitamins, add extra crunch.

broccoli & almond soup

serves 6
prep + cook time 30 minutes

25 g (1 oz) butter
1 onion, roughly chopped
500 g (1 lb) broccoli, cut into
  florets, stems sliced
40 g (1½ oz) ground almonds
900 ml (1½ pints) vegetable or
  chicken stock
300 ml (½ pint) milk
salt and pepper

to garnish
15 g (½ oz) butter
6 tablespoons natural yogurt
3 tablespoons flaked almonds

1 Heat the butter in a saucepan, add the onion and fry gently for 5 minutes until just beginning to soften. Stir in the broccoli until coated in the butter then add the ground almonds, stock and a little salt and pepper.

2 Bring to the boil then cover and simmer for 10 minutes until the broccoli is just tender and still bright green. Leave to cool slightly, then purée in batches in a blender or food processor until finely speckled with green.

3 Pour the purée back into the saucepan and stir in the milk. Reheat then taste and adjust the seasoning if needed. Heat the 15 g (½ oz) butter in a frying pan, add the almonds and fry for a few minutes, stirring until golden. Ladle the soup into bowls, drizzle a spoonful of yogurt over each bowl, then sprinkle with almonds.

For broccoli & stilton soup, omit the ground almonds. Cook as above, adding 125 g (4 oz) crumbled Stilton when reheating the soup. Stir until melted. Serve sprinkled with a little extra cheese and coarsely crushed black pepper.

courgette & dill soup

serves 8
prep + cook time 40–45 minutes

2 tablespoons olive oil
1 large onion, chopped
2 garlic cloves, crushed
1 kg (2 lb) courgettes, sliced
1.2–1.5 litres (2–2½) pints
   vegetable or chicken stock
2–4 tablespoons finely chopped
   dill
salt and pepper

to garnish
125 ml (4 fl oz) single cream
dill fronds

1 Heat the oil in a saucepan and fry the onion and garlic until soft but not browned. Add the courgettes, cover the pan with greaseproof paper and cook over a low heat for 10 minutes until the courgettes are soft. Add 1.2 litres (2 pints) of the stock, cover the pan with a lid and simmer for a further 10–15 minutes.

2 Transfer the courgettes and a little of the stock to a blender or food processor. Purée until smooth, then pour into a clean saucepan. Add the stock that the courgettes were cooked in and the remaining stock, along with the chopped dill. Season to taste with salt and pepper, then bring to the boil.

3 Serve the soup in soup bowls, garnished with a swirl of cream and dill fronds.

Tip
Canned and ready made chilled soups are often a source of hidden sugar, so make your own to keep down your daily sugar count.

spinach & red lentil soup

serves 4
prep + cook time 30 minutes

250 g (8 oz) dried red lentils
3 tablespoons olive oil
1 large onion, finely chopped
2 garlic cloves, crushed
2.5 cm (1 in) piece fresh root
   ginger, grated
1 red chilli, deseeded and
   chopped, plus extra to garnish
   (optional)
1 tablespoon medium curry
   powder
300 ml (½ pint) hot vegetable stock
200 g (7 oz) can tomatoes
100 g (3½ oz) baby leaf spinach
25 g (1 oz) chopped coriander
   leaves, plus extra to garnish
100 ml (3½ fl oz) coconut cream
salt and pepper
4 tablespoons natural yogurt,
   to serve

1 Put the lentils into a medium saucepan and cover with 900 ml (1½ pints) cold water. Bring to the boil, skimming off the scum as it rises to the surface, and leave to simmer for 10 minutes until the lentils are tender and just falling apart. Remove from the heat, cover and set aside.

2 Meanwhile, heat the oil in a large saucepan, add the onion and fry gently for 5 minutes. Add the garlic, ginger and chilli and fry for a further 2 minutes. Stir in the curry powder and ½ teaspoon pepper and cook for a further 2 minutes.

3 Add the stock, the lentils and their cooking liquid, the tomatoes, spinach and coriander and season with salt to taste. Cover and simmer for 5 minutes then add the coconut cream.

4 Whizz the mixture with a hand-held blender, until the soup is almost smooth.

5 Ladle the soup into 4 bowls and garnish each with a spoonful of yogurt, the remaining coriander leaves, pepper and finely chopped red chilli, if desired.

Tip
Filling and warming, this soup has an impressive array of ingredients from immune-boosting coconut cream to iron-rich spinach.

squash, kale & mixed bean soup

serves 6
prep + cook time 1 hour

1 tablespoon olive oil
1 onion, finely chopped
2 garlic cloves, finely chopped
1 teaspoon smoked paprika
500 g (1 lb) butternut squash,
    peeled, deseeded and diced
2 small carrots, diced
500 g (1 lb) tomatoes, skinned and
    roughly diced
410 g (13½ oz) can mixed beans,
    drained
900 ml (1½ pints) vegetable or
    chicken stock
150 ml (¼ pint) full-fat crème
    fraîche
100 g (3½ oz) kale, torn into
    bite-sized pieces
salt and pepper

1 Heat the oil in a saucepan, add the onion and fry gently for
5 minutes. Stir in the garlic and smoked paprika and cook briefly,
then add the squash, carrots, tomatoes and drained beans.
2 Pour on the stock, season with salt and pepper and bring to the
boil, stirring. Cover and simmer for 25 minutes until the vegetables
are tender.
3 Stir the crème fraîche into the soup, then add the kale, pressing it
just beneath the surface of the stock. Cover and cook for 5 minutes
until the kale has just wilted. Ladle into bowls and serve with warm
garlic bread.

lamb, chickpea & cinnamon broth

serves 4
prep + cook time 20 minutes

2 tablespoons ghee or olive oil
1 onion, finely chopped
1 garlic clove, finely chopped
1 teaspoon coriander seeds
1 teaspoon cumin seeds
2 dried red chillies
2–3 cinnamon sticks
250 g (8 oz) lean lamb, cut into
   thin strips
400 g (13 oz) can chickpeas,
   rinsed and drained
1.2 litres (2 pints) hot lamb or
   chicken stock
small bunch of flat leaf parsley,
   roughly chopped
salt and pepper
lemon wedges, to serve
   (optional)

1 Heat the ghee or oil in a heavy-based saucepan, stir in the onion, garlic and spices and cook for 2–3 minutes until the onion begins to colour.

2 Add the lamb and cook for 1–2 minutes, stirring to coat well, then add the chickpeas. Pour in the stock and bring to the boil, then cook over a medium heat for 15 minutes.

3 Stir in the parsley and season. Serve the broth with lemon wedges to squeeze over, if liked.

sweet potato, bacon & cabbage soup

serves 4
prep + cook time 40 minutes

2 onions, chopped
2 garlic cloves, sliced
4 lean back bacon rashers,
    chopped
500 g (1 lb) sweet potatoes,
    chopped
2 parsnips, chopped
1 teaspoon chopped thyme
900 ml (1½ pints) vegetable stock
1 baby savoy cabbage, shredded

1 Place the onions, garlic and bacon in a large saucepan and fry for 2–3 minutes.
2 Add the sweet potatoes, parsnips, thyme and stock, bring to the boil and simmer for 15 minutes.
3 Transfer two-thirds of the soup to a liquidizer or food processor and blend until smooth. Return to the pan, add the cabbage and continue to simmer for 5–7 minutes until the cabbage is just cooked. Serve with the Herbed Soda Breads on page 27, if liked.

For squash & broccoli soup, follow the recipe above, replacing the sweet potatoes with 500 g (1 lb) peeled and chopped butternut squash and the cabbage with 100 g (3½ oz) broccoli, broken into small florets.

summer vegetable soup

serves 4
prep + cook time 30 minutes

1 teaspoon olive oil
1 leek, thinly sliced
1 large potato, chopped
450 g (14½ oz) prepared mixed
    summer vegetables, such as
    peas, asparagus spears, broad
    beans and courgettes
2 tablespoons chopped mint,
    plus extra leaves to garnish
900 ml (1½ pints) vegetable stock
2 tablespoons crème fraîche
salt (optional) and pepper

1 Heat the oil in a medium saucepan, add the leek and potato and cook for 3–4 minutes until softened.

2 Add the mixed vegetables to the pan with the mint and stock and bring to the boil. Reduce the heat and simmer for 10 minutes.

3 Transfer the soup to a blender or food processor and blend until smooth. Return the soup to the pan and season to taste with salt, if necessary, and pepper.

4 Heat through and serve in soup bowls with the crème fraiche swirled over the top. Garnish with extra mint leaves.

For cheesy croutons, thinly slice a wholegrain baguette, cover the slices with grated Cheddar cheese and grill under a preheated hot grill for 5 minutes until golden and bubbling. Serve on top of hot soup.

lime & coconut squid salad

serves 2
prep + cook time 20 minutes

10–12 prepared baby squid, about
    375 g (12 oz) including tentacles,
    cleaned
4 limes, halved
mixed salad leaves

dressing
2 red chillies, deseeded and finely
    chopped
finely grated rind and juice of
    2 limes
2.5 cm (1 inch) piece of fresh root
    ginger, peeled and grated
100 g (3½ oz) freshly grated
    coconut
4 tablespoons groundnut oil
1–2 tablespoons chilli oil
1 tablespoon white wine vinegar

1 Cut down the side of each squid so that they can be laid flat on a chopping board. Using a sharp knife, lightly score the inside flesh in a crisscross pattern.

2 Mix all the dressing ingredients together in a bowl. Toss the squid in half the dressing until thoroughly coated.

3 Heat a ridged griddle pan until smoking hot, add the limes, cut side down, and cook for 2 minutes or until well charred. Remove from the pan and set aside. Keeping the griddle pan very hot, add the squid pieces and cook for 1 minute. Turn them over and cook for a further minute or until they turn white, lose their transparency and are charred.

4 Transfer the squid to a chopping board and cut into strips. Drizzle with the remaining dressing and serve immediately with the charred limes and a salad of mixed leaves.

warm scallop, parsnip & carrot salad

serves 4
prep + cook time 45 minutes

4 carrots, quartered lengthways
3 parsnips, quartered lengthways
2 tablespoons olive oil
1 tablespoon cumin seeds
12 fresh king scallops
2 tablespoons lemon juice
salt and pepper
chopped parsley, to garnish

dressing
4 tablespoons natural yogurt
2 tablespoons lemon juice
2 tablespoons olive oil
1 teaspoon ground cumin

1 Put the carrots and parsnips on a foil-lined baking sheet. Drizzle with 1 tablespoon of the oil, scatter over the cumin seeds, season with salt and pepper and cook in a preheated oven, 180°C (350°F), Gas Mark 4, for 20–25 minutes.

2 Meanwhile, make the dressing. Mix the yogurt, lemon juice, oil and ground cumin in a small bowl. Season to taste with salt and pepper.

3 Trim the scallops to remove the tough muscle on the outside of the white fleshy part. Heat the remaining oil in a large frying pan and fry the scallops for 2 minutes on each side until they are just cooked through. Pour over the lemon juice and transfer the scallops and cooking juices to a large salad bowl.

4 Add the carrots and parsnips to the bowl and mix, then transfer them to a serving dish, spoon over the yogurt dressing, garnish with parsley and serve.

smoked mackerel salad with orange & avocado

serves 4
prep time 10 minutes

4 peppered smoked mackerel
    fillets, skin removed
2 small oranges
2 tablespoons avocado oil
175 g (6 oz) rocket and watercress
    salad
2 ripe avocados, peeled, stoned
    and sliced
50 g (2 oz) walnut halves (optional)
salt and pepper

1 Flake the smoked mackerel fillets.
2 Using a sharp knife, cut the top and bottom off each orange. Slice away the skin and pith, then cut into segments, slicing either side of the membrane. Squeeze out the membrane before discarding it, then pour all the juice into a bowl.
3 Place 3 tablespoons of the reserved juice in another bowl, add the avocado oil, salt and pepper and whisk together.
4 Combine the salad leaves gently with the flaked mackerel, orange segments and avocado, and arrange attractively on serving plates. Scatter over the walnuts, if using, then drizzle over the dressing to serve.

Tip
Rich in protein, mackerel is also an excellent source of omega-3 to protect the heart and vitamin D for strong teeth and bones.

lentil & feta salad

serves 2–4
prep + cook time 45 minutes

250 g (8 oz) Puy lentils
2 carrots, finely diced
2 celery sticks, finely diced
100 g (3½ oz) feta cheese
2 tablespoons chopped parsley

dressing
3 tablespoons white wine vinegar
2 teaspoons Dijon mustard
5 tablespoons olive oil
salt and pepper

1 Put the lentils in a saucepan, cover with cold water and add a pinch of salt. Bring to the boil and cook for 20–25 minutes until just cooked but not mushy. Drain and refresh in cold water, then drain again and transfer to a large salad bowl.

2 Add the carrots and celery to the bowl with the lentils. Crumble in the feta and add the chopped parsley.

3 Make the dressing by whisking the vinegar, mustard and oil. Add the dressing to the salad and stir to combine well. Season to taste with salt and pepper and serve immediately.

Tip
Avoid using sugary balsamic vinegar and bottled salad dressings and make your own, like this easy, sugar-free vinaigrette recipe above.

buckwheat & salmon salad

serves 4
prep + cook time 35 minutes

300 g (10 oz) buckwheat
250 g (8 oz) broccoli florets
250 g (8 oz) cherry tomatoes,
    halved
250 g (8 oz) smoked salmon
small bunch of parsley, chopped
4 tablespoons chopped dill
salt and pepper

dressing
juice of 1 lemon
3 tablespoons olive oil

1 Put the buckwheat in a saucepan, cover with cold water and add a pinch of salt. Bring to the boil and cook for 10–15 minutes until still firm and not mushy. Drain under running cold water and remove the foam that accumulates. Drain again when cool.

2 Bring a large saucepan of lightly salted water to the boil and blanch the broccoli florets for 2–3 minutes. Refresh in cold water and drain.

3 Mix the cherry tomatoes with the buckwheat and broccoli in a large salad bowl. Slice the smoked salmon and add it to the bowl with the parsley and half of the dill.

4 Make the dressing by whisking the lemon juice and oil. Pour the dressing over the salad, mix lightly to combine and season to taste with salt and pepper.

quinoa, courgette & pomegranate salad

serves 4
prep + cook time 20 minutes

75 g (3 oz) quinoa
1 large courgette
1 tablespoon white wine vinegar
4 tablespoons olive oil
4 spring onions, finely sliced
100 g (3½ oz) cherry tomatoes,
　halved
1 red chilli, finely chopped
100 g (3½ oz) pomegranate seeds
　(or seeds of ½ pomegranate)
small handful of finely chopped
　flat leaf parsley
salt and pepper

1 Cook the quinoa following the packet instructions then drain and rinse under cold water. Drain again.
2 Cut the ends off the courgette then cut into ribbons using a potato peeler.
3 Whisk together the vinegar and 2 tablespoons of the oil and season with salt and pepper.
4 Put the rest of the ingredients in a large bowl, then pour over the dressing and toss everything together and serve.

Tip
In recognition of the numerous health benefits of protein-rich quinoa, the United Nations named 2013 International Quinoa Year!

squash & pumpkin seed salad

serves 4–6
prep + cook time 25–30 minutes
+ cooling time

1 tablespoon olive oil
1 small butternut squash, peeled,
    deseeded and sliced
200 g (7 oz) baby spinach leaves
50 g (2 oz) feta cheese, crumbled
25 g (1 oz) pumpkin seeds

dressing
large handful of coriander leaves
1 green chilli, deseeded, if liked,
    and finely chopped
grated rind and juice of 1 lime
5 tablespoons olive oil
salt and pepper

1 Rub the oil over the squash slices. Heat a griddle pan until smoking hot, add the squash slices in batches and cook for 7–10 minutes, turning once, until lightly charred and just cooked through. Leave to cool.

2 Make the dressing by mixing together the coriander, chilli, lime rind and a little of the lime juice in a bowl. Stir in the oil, then add more lime juice if needed and season well.

3 Arrange the spinach leaves and cooled squash on a serving plate. Drizzle over the dressing, then scatter with the feta and pumpkin seeds and serve.

spicy quinoa, broad bean & avocado salad

serves 4
prep + cook time 30 minutes

200 g (7 oz) quinoa
800 ml (1 pint 8 fl oz) hot vegetable
   stock
500 g (1 lb) podded broad beans
1 tablespoon cumin seeds
3 lemons
2 ripe avocados
2 garlic cloves, crushed
2 red chillies, deseeded if liked
   and finely chopped
200 g (7 oz) radishes, thickly sliced
small handful of chopped
   coriander leaves
5 tablespoons extra-virgin olive oil
salt and pepper

1 Put the quinoa in a sieve and rinse well, then put in a medium saucepan and add the stock. Bring to the boil, then reduce the heat to medium and simmer for 10–12 minutes, uncovered, until the germ separates and most of the stock has been absorbed. Drain well, then leave to cool.

2 Meanwhile, cook the broad beans in a saucepan of boiling water for 1–2 minutes. Drain, then put in a bowl of cold water and leave the beans to cool slightly. Drain again, then slip off and discard the skins and set the beans aside.

3 Heat a frying pan until hot, add the cumin seeds and dry-fry over a medium heat until lightly brown, then remove from the pan and set aside. When cooled, lightly crush the seeds.

4 Remove the peel and pith from the lemons and cut each one into segments, discarding any seeds, then put into a large bowl. Squeeze any remaining juices into the bowl.

5 Peel, stone and thickly slice the avocados, add to the bowl and toss in the lemon juice. Add the drained quinoa, broad beans, toasted cumin seeds and the remaining ingredients, then season. Toss to mix well and serve.

Tip
Quinoa is a real powerhouse of nutrition, offering protein, calcium, manganese, B vitamins and vitamin E.

pink grapefruit & fennel salad

serves 4
prep time 30 minutes

1 fennel bulb
1 tablespoon olive oil
juice of ½ lemon
1 scant teaspoon cumin seeds,
   crushed
2 pink grapefruit
1 scant teaspoon salt
2–3 spring onions, finely sliced
1 tablespoon black olives, pitted

1 Cut the base off the fennel and remove the outer layers. Cut in half lengthways and in half horizontally, then finely slice with the grain. Place in a bowl and toss with the oil, lemon juice and cumin seeds. Leave to marinate for 20 minutes.

2 Meanwhile, using a sharp knife, remove the peel and pith from the grapefruit. Holding the grapefruit over a bowl to catch the juice, cut down between the membranes and remove the segments. Cut each segment in half, place in the bowl and sprinkle with the salt. Leave to stand for 5 minutes to draw out the sweet juices.

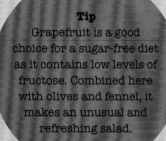

Tip
Grapefruit is a good choice for a sugar-free diet as it contains low levels of fructose. Combined here with olives and fennel, it makes an unusual and refreshing salad.

crunchy vegetable salad

serves 4–6
prep time 10 minutes + standing time

½ head of white cabbage, thinly sliced
2 carrots, thinly sliced
75 g (3 oz) radishes, thinly sliced
2 spring onions, thinly sliced
1 bunch of coriander, chopped

dressing
1 teaspoon cumin seeds
1 red chilli, deseeded, if liked, and finely chopped
 grated rind and juice of 2 limes
2 tablespoons olive oil
salt and pepper

1 Make the dressing by mixing together all the ingredients in a bowl. Season well.
2 Place all the salad ingredients in a serving bowl, then toss together with the dressing. Leave to stand for 5 minutes before serving.

Tip
Ready made coleslaw often contains added sugar and is laden with mayonnaise. Why not try this spicy, sugar-free salad at your next barbecue instead?

soft boiled egg & bacon salad

serves 4
prep + cook time 20 minutes

4 thick slices of day-old bread
6 tablespoons olive oil
4 eggs
1 tablespoon Dijon mustard
juice of ½ lemon
100 g (3½ oz) streaky bacon, cut
   into bite-sized pieces
100 g (3½ oz) rocket leaves
salt and pepper

1 Cut the bread into small bite-sized pieces and toss in 2 tablespoons of the oil. Spread out on a baking sheet and bake in a preheated oven, 200°C (400°F), Gas Mark 6, for 10 minutes or until golden brown.

2 Meanwhile, cook the eggs in a saucepan of boiling water for 4 minutes. Drain, then cool under cold running water for 1 minute.

3 Whisk together the remaining oil, mustard and lemon juice in a small bowl.

4 Heat a nonstick frying pan, add the bacon and cook over a medium heat for 5 minutes until crisp and golden. Put into a bowl with the rocket.

5 Shell the eggs, then roughly break in half and add to the bacon and rocket. Scatter over the croûtons, then drizzle over the dressing, season to taste with salt and pepper and serve immediately.

For creamy yogurt dressing, to replace the mustard dressing, whisk together 4 tablespoons olive oil, the juice of 1 lemon, 6 tablespoons natural yogurt, 1 crushed garlic clove and 1 teaspoon dried oregano.

smoked chicken salad

serves 4
prep time 10 minutes

50 g (2 oz) pumpkin seeds
300 g (10 oz) skinless smoked
  chicken breast, shredded
2 red onions, finely sliced and
  rinsed in water
150 g (5 oz) cherry tomatoes,
  halved
75 g (3 oz) mixed salad leaves

dressing
1 ripe avocado, peeled, stoned
  and diced
2 tablespoons lime juice
1 tablespoon Dijon mustard
salt and pepper

1 Heat a small frying pan until hot, add the pumpkin seeds and dry-fry for 1–2 minutes, stirring occasionally, until golden.
2 Make the dressing by placing all the ingredients in a food processor and blending them until smooth. Season to taste.
3 Place the chicken, onions, tomatoes, pumpkin seeds and salad leaves in a salad bowl and toss together. Drizzle over the dressing and serve with crusty bread, if liked.

warm chicken, veg & bulgar salad

serves 4
prep + cook time 30 minutes

6 tablespoons olive oil
1 large courgette, cut into thick
  slices
1 large red onion, cut into slim
  wedges
1 red pepper, cored, deseeded
  and cut into chunks
½ small aubergine, cut into small
  chunks
1 garlic clove, thinly sliced
150 g (5 oz) bulgar wheat
4 boneless, skinless chicken
  breasts, about 200 g (7 oz) each
4 tablespoons chopped parsley
salt and pepper

1 Heat 5 tablespoons of the oil in a large frying pan, add the courgette, onion, red pepper, aubergine and garlic and cook over a high heat for 15–20 minutes, stirring almost continuously, until golden and softened.

2 Meanwhile, cook the bulgar wheat in a saucepan of lightly salted boiling water for 15 minutes until tender.

3 While the bulgar wheat is cooking, brush the remaining oil over the chicken breasts and season well. Heat a large griddle pan until smoking, add the chicken and cook over a high heat for 4–5 minutes on each side, or until golden and cooked through. Remove from the heat and thinly slice diagonally.

4 Drain the bulgar wheat. Place in a large bowl, toss with the parsley and season. Add the hot vegetables and chicken, toss together and serve.

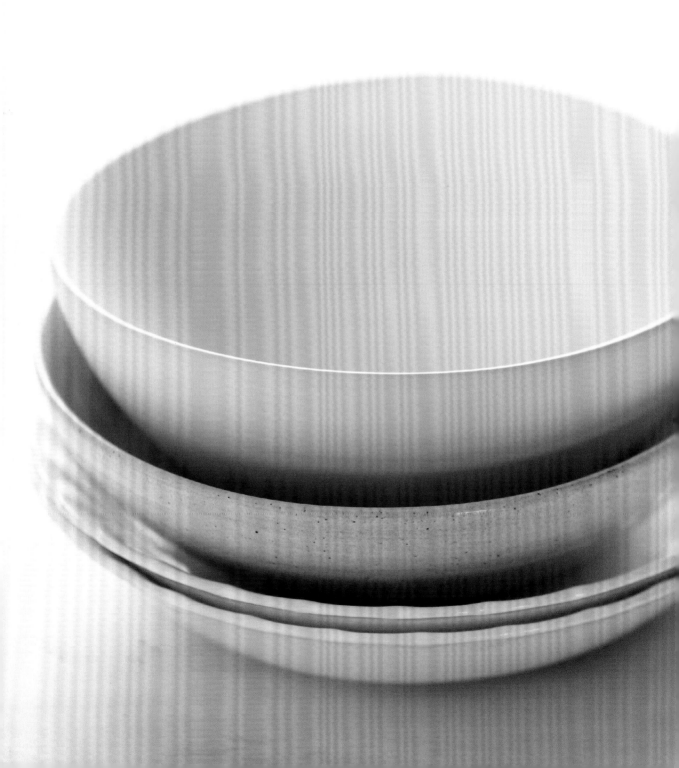

lunches &
light meals

garlic mushrooms on sourdough toast

serves 4
prep + cook time 15 minutes

25 g (1 oz) butter
3 tablespoons olive oil, plus extra
    to serve
750 g (1½ lb) mixed mushrooms,
    such as oyster, shiitake, flat and
    button, trimmed and sliced
2 garlic cloves, crushed
1 tablespoon chopped thyme
grated rind and juice of 1 lemon
2 tablespoons chopped parsley
4 slices of sourdough bread
100 g (3½ oz) mixed salad leaves
salt and pepper
fresh Parmesan cheese shavings,
    to serve

1 Melt the butter with the oil in a large frying pan. As soon as the butter stops foaming, add the mushrooms, garlic, thyme, lemon rind and salt and pepper and cook over a medium heat, stirring, for 4–5 minutes until tender. Scatter over the parsley and squeeze over a little lemon juice.
2 Meanwhile, toast the bread, then arrange it on serving plates.
3 Top the sourdough toast with an equal quantity of the salad leaves and mushrooms, and drizzle over a little more oil and lemon juice. Scatter with Parmesan shavings and serve immediately.

For mushrooms with camembert on toast, brush 8 large mushrooms with olive oil and grill for 4–5 minutes each side. Place on 4 slices of sourdough toast and top with 2 slices of camembert. Grill for 2–3 minutes until the cheese melts.

asparagus, tomato & feta frittata

serves 4
prep + cook time about 50 minutes
+ cooling time

3 tablespoons olive oil, plus extra
   for oiling
2 leeks, thinly sliced
1 garlic clove, crushed
250 g (8 oz) asparagus, trimmed
6 eggs
100 g (3½ oz) feta cheese, diced
4 tablespoons freshly grated
   Parmesan cheese
175 g (6 oz) cherry tomatoes
salt and pepper

1 Heat the oil in a frying pan, add the leeks and garlic and cook over a medium heat, stirring frequently, for 10 minutes until tender. Cool.

2 Cook the asparagus in a large saucepan of lightly salted boiling water for 2 minutes. Drain, refresh under cold water and pat dry. Cut into 5 cm (2 inch) lengths.

3 Lightly oil a 20 cm (8 inch) square baking dish with olive oil and line the base with nonstick baking paper. Beat the eggs in a bowl and stir in the leek mixture, asparagus, feta, half the Parmesan and salt and pepper. Pour the mixture into the prepared dish and top with the tomatoes. Sprinkle over the remaining Parmesan and bake in a preheated oven, 190°C (375°F), Gas Mark 5, for 25–30 minutes until puffed up and firm in the centre.

4 Leave to cool in the dish for 10 minutes, then turn out on to a board and serve warm with a crisp green salad.

baked sweet potatoes

serves 4
prep + cook time 50–55 minutes

4 sweet potatoes, about 250 g
   (8 oz) each, scrubbed
200 g (7 oz) soured cream
2 spring onions, trimmed and
   finely chopped
1 tablespoon chopped chives
50 g (2 oz) butter
salt and pepper

1 Put the potatoes in a roasting tin and roast in a preheated oven, 220°C (425°F), Gas Mark 7, for 45–50 minutes until cooked through.
2 Meanwhile, combine the soured cream, spring onions, chives and salt and pepper in a bowl.
3 Cut the baked potatoes in half lengthways, top with the butter and spoon over the soured cream mixture. Serve immediately.

For crispy sweet potato skins, allow the baked sweet potatoes to cool, cut into wedges and remove some of the soft potato, leaving a good lining on the skin. Deep fry in hot oil for 4–5 minutes until crisp. Serve with soured cream to dip.

spiced courgette fritters

serves 4
prep + cook time 25 minutes

100 g (3½ oz) gram flour (besan)
1 teaspoon baking powder
½ teaspoon ground turmeric
2 teaspoons ground coriander
1 teaspoon ground cumin
1 teaspoon chilli powder
250 ml (8 fl oz) soda water, chilled
625 g (1¼ lb) courgettes, cut into
   thick batons
salt
sunflower oil, for deep frying
natural yogurt, to dip

1 Sift the gram flour, baking powder, turmeric, coriander, cumin and chilli powder into a large mixing bowl. Season with salt and gradually add the soda water to make a thick batter, being careful not to overmix.
2 Pour sunflower oil into a wok until one-third full and heat to 180–190°C (350–375°F), or until a cube of bread browns in 30 seconds.
3 Dip the courgette batons in the spiced batter and then deep-fry in batches for 1–2 minutes or until crisp and golden. Remove with a slotted spoon and drain on kitchen paper. Serve the courgettes immediately with thick natural yogurt, to dip.

For spicy raita, whisk 200 g (7 oz) natural yogurt until smooth. Add 6 tablespoons finely chopped mint, 1 small green chilli, deseeded and finely chopped, ½ teaspoon ground cumin and salt to taste. Sprinkle with chilli to serve.

quick supper dishes

stilton welsh rarebit

serves 2   **prep + cook time** 10 minutes

15 g (½ oz) butter
4 spring onions, sliced
100 g (4 oz) Stilton cheese, crumbled
1 egg yolk
a little milk
2 slices of granary bread, lightly toasted
2 slices of bacon, grilled

1 Heat the butter in a small saucepan and fry the spring onions for 2–3 minutes until softened. Leave to cool, then mix with the Stilton and egg yolk, adding enough milk to make a spreadable mixture.
2 Spread the mixture over the toast and cook under a preheated hot grill for about 2 minutes until golden and bubbling. Serve topped with the grilled bacon.

feta, herb & rocket frittata

serves 2   **prep + cook time** 15 minutes

4 eggs, beaten
2 tablespoons chopped herbs, such as chives, chervil and parsley
1 tablespoon double cream
1 tablespoon olive oil
1 small red onion, finely sliced
½ red pepper, deseeded and finely sliced
100 g (3½ oz) feta cheese
large handful of rocket leaves
salt and black pepper

1 Beat together the eggs, herbs and cream.
2 Heat the oil in a nonstick frying pan with an ovenproof handle, add the onion and pepper and fry for 3–4 minutes until just soft. Add the egg mixture and cook for about 3 minutes until almost set.
3 Crumble over the feta, then cook under a preheated hot grill until golden. Top with the rocket.

spiced tuna open sandwiches

serves 4   **prep time** 10 minutes

2 x 250 g (8 oz) cans tuna, drained
4 tablespoons mayonnaise
2 tablespoons sliced celery
¼ teaspoon smoked paprika
¼ teaspoon cayenne pepper
1 tablespoon finely chopped red onion
juice of ½ lemon
¼ cucumber, thinly sliced
4 slices of pumperknickel bread
a few sprigs of watercress
lemon wedges, to serve

1 Flake the tuna in a bowl, then mix together with the mayonnaise, celery, paprika, cayenne pepper, onion and lemon juice.
2 Arrange the slices of cucumber on the pumpernickel, then top with the tuna mixture. Top with a few sprigs of watercress.
3 Serve with lemon wedges.

ricotta-stuffed mushrooms

serves 2   **prep time** 9–10 minutes

4 large flat chestnut or portobello mushrooms
2 tablespoons garlic-infused olive oil
salt and pepper
200 g (7 oz) ricotta cheese
12 large basil leaves, roughly chopped
finely grated rind of 1 lemon
25 g (1 oz) Parmesan cheese, grated
25 g (1 oz) pine nuts

1 Remove the stalks from the mushrooms and brush all over with the oil. Season to taste and place on a baking sheet, skin side up. Cook under a preheated hot grill for 5 minutes.
2 Meanwhile, mix all the remaining ingredients in a bowl and season to taste. Turn the mushrooms and pile the filling into the cavities, pressing it down.
3 Cook for a further 3–4 minutes until the filling is golden and the mushrooms are cooked through. Serve immediately with a rocket salad, if liked.

pea & leek omelette

serves 4
prep + cook time 25–28 minutes

250 g (8 oz) baby new potatoes
75 g (3 oz) butter
1 tablespoon olive oil
500 g (1 lb) leeks, trimmed,
   cleaned and cut into 1 cm
   (½ inch) slices
200 g (7 oz) frozen or fresh peas
6 eggs
150 ml (5 fl oz) milk
2 tablespoons chopped chives
125 g (4 oz) soft garlic and chive
   cheese
salt and pepper

1 Cook the potatoes in boiling water for about 10 minutes or until cooked but still firm.
2 Meanwhile, melt the butter with the oil in a large frying pan, add the leeks, cover and cook, stirring frequently, for 8–10 minutes or until soft. Stir in the peas.
3 Drain the potatoes, cut them into quarters and add to the frying pan. Continue cooking for 2–3 minutes.
4 Whisk the eggs with the milk and chives, season well and pour into the frying pan. Move around with a spatula so that the vegetables are well coated and the egg begins to cook. Crumble the cheese on top and leave over a medium heat for 2–3 minutes until the egg becomes firm.
5 Place under a preheated hot grill for 3–4 minutes until the omelette is completely set and the top is golden brown. Serve in thick slices with a green salad and dressing, if liked.

Tip
Versatile eggs are in the top 10 of nutritious foods. An egg contains only around 75 calories but has about 7 g of protein, along with vitamins and minerals.

baked cabbage with nuts & cheese

serves 4
prep + cook time 45 minutes

375 g (12 oz) white cabbage,
    shredded
125 g (4 oz) green or savoy
    cabbage, shredded
1 teaspoon ground nutmeg
125 g (4 oz) roasted unsalted
    peanuts, toasted
25 g (1 oz) butter
25 g (1 oz) plain flour
450 ml (¾ pint) milk
125 g (4 oz) strong Cheddar
    cheese, grated
1 teaspoon Dijon mustard
2 tablespoons chopped parsley
25 g (1 oz) wholemeal
    breadcrumbs

1 Cook the two types of cabbage in boiling water for 5 minutes until just tender. Drain and place in a large mixing bowl and toss with the nutmeg and peanuts.

2 Heat the butter in a nonstick saucepan until melted. Remove from the heat, add the flour and mix to a paste. Return to the heat and cook for a few seconds. Remove from the heat and add the milk a little at a time, stirring well between each addition. Return to the heat and bring to the boil, stirring continuously until boiled and thickened.

3 Remove the pan from the heat and add 75 g (3 oz) of the grated Cheddar and the mustard. Mix well, pour over the cabbage and mix in.

4 Transfer the mixture to a gratin dish, or 4 individual gratin dishes. Toss the remaining cheese with the parsley and breadcrumbs, then sprinkle over the top and bake in a preheated oven, 200°C (400°F), Gas Mark 6, for 20 minutes until golden and bubbling.

For root vegetable bake with nuts & cheese, replace the cabbage with 375 g (12 oz) sliced butternut squash and 250 g (8 oz) sliced parsnips cooked in boiling water for 5 minutes and drained.

peppered beef with salad leaves

serves 6
prep + cook time 25 minutes

2 thick-cut sirloin steaks, about
    500 g (1 lb) in total
3 teaspoons coloured
    peppercorns, coarsely crushed
coarse salt flakes
200 g (7 oz) natural yogurt
1–1½ teaspoons horseradish
    sauce (to taste)
1 garlic clove, crushed
150 g (5 oz) mixed green salad
    leaves
100 g (3½ oz) button mushrooms,
    sliced
1 red onion, thinly sliced
1 tablespoon olive oil
salt and pepper

1 Trim the fat from the steaks and rub the meat with the crushed peppercorns and salt flakes.

2 Mix together the yogurt, horseradish sauce and garlic and season to taste with salt and pepper. Add the salad leaves, mushrooms and most of the red onion and toss gently.

3 Heat the oil in a frying pan, add the steaks and cook over a high heat for 2 minutes until browned. Turn over and cook for 2 minutes for medium rare, 3–4 minutes for medium or 5 minutes for well done.

4 Spoon the salad leaves into the centre of six serving plates. Thinly slice the steaks and arrange the pieces on top, then garnish with the remaining red onion.

chicken skewers with spiced chickpea mash

serves 4
prep + cook time 20 minutes

3 chicken breasts, each about
   150 g (5 oz), cut into small
   chunks
3 tablespoons sesame oil
1 tablespoon chopped thyme
   leaves
2 tablespoons sesame seeds
2 tablespoons olive oil
1 onion, chopped
1 small red chilli, deseeded if liked
   and chopped
2 thyme sprigs, plus extra to
   garnish (optional)
2 × 400 g (13 oz) cans chickpeas,
   rinsed and drained
6 tablespoons hot chicken stock
salt and pepper

1 Put the chicken pieces in a bowl with the sesame oil, thyme leaves and sesame seeds and toss to coat. Thread the chicken evenly on to 8 skewers and arrange on a foil-lined grill rack. Place under a preheated grill, turning frequently, for 10 minutes or until golden and cooked through.

2 Meanwhile, heat the oil in a heavy-based frying pan and cook the onion, chilli and thyme sprigs over a moderately high heat for 3–4 minutes or until the onion is soft and becoming golden. Add the chickpeas. Heat, stirring, for 1 minute, then add the stock, cover the pan with a lid, bring to the boil and cook for 3 minutes until piping hot. Season well. Transfer to a food processor or blender and process until almost smooth but still holding some texture.

3 Spoon the chickpea purée on to serving plates and top each with a chicken skewer. Garnish with thyme sprigs, if liked.

Tip
Chickpea mash has a lower GI level than classic mashed potato. It is also excellent served with lamb chops, roast chicken and sausages.

greek-style summer omelette

serves 4
prep + cook time 30 minutes

8 large eggs
1 teaspoon dried oregano
1 tablespoon finely chopped mint
4 tablespoons finely chopped flat
    leaf parsley
2 tablespoons olive oil
2 small red onions, peeled and
    roughly chopped
2 large ripe tomatoes, roughly
    chopped
½ courgette, roughly chopped
100 g (3½ oz) black olives, pitted
100 g (3½ oz) feta cheese
salt and pepper

1 Whisk the eggs in a bowl and add the oregano, mint and parsley. Season well.

2 Heat the oil in a large nonstick frying pan. Add the red onion and fry over a high heat for about 3–4 minutes or until brown around the edges. Add the tomatoes, courgette and olives and cook for 3–4 minutes or until the vegetables begin to soften.

3 Meanwhile, preheat the grill to medium-high. Reduce the heat to medium and pour the eggs into the frying pan. Cook for 3–4 minutes, stirring as they begin to set, until they are firm but still slightly runny in places.

4 Scatter over the feta, then place the pan under the preheated grill for 4–5 minutes or until the omelette is puffed up and golden. Cut into wedges and serve with a crisp green salad, if liked.

For classic greek salad, thinly slice 2 red onions, 4 tomatoes and 1 cucumber. Add 200 g (7 oz) cubed feta cheese and 100 g (3½ oz) pitted black olives. Sprinkle with 6 tablespoons of olive oil and 1 teaspoon dried oregano. Season and mix well.

moroccan baked eggs

serves 2
prep + cook time 35–45 minutes

½ tablespoon olive oil
½ onion, chopped
1 garlic clove, sliced
½ teaspoon ras el hanout
pinch of ground cinnamon
½ teaspoon ground coriander
400 g (13 oz) cherry tomatoes
2 tablespoons chopped coriander
2 eggs
salt and pepper

1 Heat the oil in a frying pan, add the onion and garlic and cook for 6–7 minutes until softened and lightly golden. Stir in the spices and cook, stirring, for a further 1 minute.

2 Add the tomatoes and season well with salt and pepper, then simmer gently for 8–10 minutes.

3 Scatter over 1 tablespoon of the coriander, then divide the mixture between 2 individual ovenproof dishes. Break an egg into each dish.

4 Bake in a preheated oven, 220°C (425°F), Gas Mark 7, for 8–10 minutes until the egg whites are set but the yolks are still slightly runny. Cook for a further 2–3 minutes if you prefer the eggs to be cooked through. Serve scattered with the remaining coriander.

family
favourites

gingered chicken, seed & vegetable rice

serves 4
prep + cook time 20 minutes

250 g (8 oz) easy-cook brown rice
2 tablespoons olive oil
300 g (10 oz) diced chicken
1 tablespoon ginger paste
1 onion, thinly sliced
4 tablespoons sunflower seeds
3 tablespoons pumpkin seeds
1 tablespoon black mustard seeds
1 large courgette, grated
1 large carrot, grated
175 g (6 oz) petit pois

1 Cook the rice in a large saucepan of lightly salted boiling water for 15 minutes or until tender.

2 Meanwhile, put 1 tablespoon of the oil in a large mixing bowl with the chicken and ginger paste and mix well to lightly coat the chicken. Add the chicken and onion to a large, heavy-based frying pan and cook, stirring occasionally, for 10 minutes or until golden in places and cooked through.

3 Meanwhile, in a separate pan heat the remaining oil and cook the seeds for 1 minute to brown a little. Add the courgette and carrot and stir-fry for 3 minutes until softened, then add the petit pois and stir-fry for a further 2–3 minutes until piping hot.

4 Drain the rice and add to the pan with the chicken. Toss well then add the hot seeds, courgette, carrot and petit pois and toss again. Serve hot in warmed serving bowls.

Tip
Brown rice is more nutritious than white because it is less processed and contains more nutrients and fibre. This dish would work equally well with turkey, instead of the chicken, and with quinoa in place of the rice.

spinach & chicken curry

serves 4

prep + cook time 1 hour 15 minutes
+ marinating time

5 tablespoons natural yogurt
2 tablespoons finely grated garlic
2 tablespoons peeled and finely
   grated fresh root ginger
1 tablespoon ground coriander
1 tablespoon medium curry powder
750 g (1½ lb) skinless chicken breast
   fillets, cubed
400 g (13 oz) frozen spinach
1 tablespoon groundnut oil
1 onion, finely chopped
2 teaspoons cumin seeds
400 ml (14 fl oz) chicken stock
1 tablespoon lemon juice
salt and pepper

1 Mix the yogurt, garlic, ginger, coriander and curry powder in a large non-metallic bowl. Season to taste and add the chicken. Toss to mix well, cover and marinate in the refrigerator for 8–10 hours.

2 Place the frozen spinach in a saucepan and cook over a medium heat for 6–8 minutes until defrosted. Season to taste and drain thoroughly. Transfer to a food processor and blend until smooth.

3 Heat the oil in a large nonstick frying pan over a low heat. Add the onion and fry gently for 10–12 minutes until soft and translucent. Add the cumin seeds and stir-fry for 1 minute until fragrant. Increase the heat to high, and add the chicken mixture. Stir-fry for 6–8 minutes.

4 Pour in the stock and spinach purée and bring to the boil. Reduce the heat, cover and simmer gently for 25–30 minutes until the chicken is cooked through. Uncover the pan, season to taste and cook over a high heat for 3–4 minutes, stirring often. Remove from the heat and stir in the lemon juice. Serve immediately.

thai chicken curry

serves 4
prep + cook time 30 minutes

1 tablespoon sunflower oil
1 lemon grass stalk, cut into 4 pieces
2 kaffir lime leaves, halved
1–2 red chillies, deseeded,
    if liked, then finely chopped
2.5 cm (1 inch) piece of fresh root
    ginger, peeled and grated
1 onion, finely chopped
1 garlic clove, crushed
1 red pepper, cored, deseeded and
    chopped
1 green pepper, cored, deseeded
    and chopped
3 boneless, skinless chicken breasts,
    about 500 g (1 lb) in total, chopped
410 g (13½ oz) can coconut milk
150 ml (¼ pint) chicken stock
2 tablespoons chopped fresh
    coriander leaves
salt and pepper

1 Heat the oil in a saucepan, add the lemon grass, lime leaves, chilli, ginger, onion and garlic and fry for 2 minutes. Add the red and green peppers and chopped chicken and fry for 5 minutes.

2 Pour in the coconut milk and the stock and bring to the boil, then reduce the heat and simmer for 10 minutes, or until the chicken is cooked through.

3 Stir in the coriander leaves and season to taste with salt and pepper. Serve with basmati rice, if liked.

chicken & barley risotto

serves 4
prep + cook time 1 hour 25 minutes

2 tablespoons olive oil
6 boneless, skinless chicken thighs,
    diced
1 onion, roughly chopped
2 garlic cloves, finely chopped
200 g (7 oz) chestnut mushrooms,
    sliced
250 g (8 oz) pearl barley
200 ml (7 fl oz) red wine
1.2 litres (2 pints) chicken stock
salt and pepper

to garnish
parsley, chopped
shavings of Parmesan cheese

1 Heat the oil in a large frying pan, add the chicken and onion and fry for 5 minutes, stirring until lightly browned.
2 Stir in the garlic and mushrooms and fry for 2 minutes, then mix in the barley. Add the red wine, half the stock and plenty of seasoning, then bring to the boil, stirring. Cover and simmer for 1 hour, topping up with extra stock as needed until the barley is soft.
3 Spoon into shallow bowls and garnish with the parsley and Parmesan. Serve with a green salad, if liked.

green chicken kebabs

serves 4
prep + cook time 25–27 minutes

100 ml (3½ fl oz) natural yogurt
2 garlic cloves, crushed
2 teaspoons finely grated fresh root
   ginger
2 teaspoons ground cumin
1 teaspoon ground coriander
1 green chilli, deseeded and finely
   chopped
large handful of chopped coriander
small handful of chopped mint
4 tablespoons lime juice
4 skinless, boneless chicken
   breasts, cubed
salt

1 Place the yogurt, garlic, ginger, cumin, ground coriander, chilli, chopped herbs and lime juice in a blender or food processor and blend until fairly smooth. Season lightly.

2 Place the chicken in a large mixing bowl, pour over the spice mixture and toss to coat evenly. Cover and chill until required.

3 When ready to cook, thread the chicken pieces on to 8 bamboo skewers. Cook under a preheated medium-hot grill for 8–10 minutes, turning frequently, until cooked through and lightly browned.

4 Serve immediately with a cucumber salad, with lime wedges for squeezing, if liked.

For green cod steaks, omit the chicken and yogurt and mix all the ingredients together. Use to coat four 175 g (6 oz) cod steaks, drizzle with olive oil, bake in a preheated oven, 190°C (375°F), Gas Mark 5, for 15–18 minutes.

cajun-spiced turkey meatballs

serves 4
prep + cook time 30 minutes

1 kg (2 lb) sweet potatoes, cut into
   thin wedges
4 tablespoons olive oil
1 small red onion, sliced
1 red pepper, deseeded and sliced
2 garlic cloves
4 teaspoons Cajun-style spice blend
680 g (1 lb 6 oz) jar passata
salt and pepper
soured cream, to serve (optional)

for the meatballs
500 g (1 lb) minced turkey
2 teaspoons Cajun-style spice blend
2 spring onions, finely chopped
50 g (2 oz) fresh breadcrumbs
2 tablespoons chopped coriander

1 Place the sweet potatoes in a roasting tin with half the oil and season. Toss well, then roast in a preheated oven, 220°C (425°F), Gas Mark 7, for 20–25 minutes, until golden and tender.

2 Meanwhile, combine all the meatball ingredients in a bowl, adding some salt and pepper. Roll into 20–24 balls. Heat the remaining oil in a large pan and cook the meatballs over a medium-high heat for 3–4 minutes, shaking the pan occasionally, until browned. Transfer to a plate and set aside.

3 Return the oily pan to the heat and cook the onion, pepper and garlic for 7–8 minutes, until softened and lightly coloured. Add the spice mix and stir over a medium heat for 1 minute. Pour in the passata, add a pinch of salt, pepper and sugar and simmer for 5–6 minutes to thicken slightly.

4 Add the meatballs to the sauce and simmer for a further 6–7 minutes, until cooked and the sauce has thickened. Serve with the sweet potato wedges and a dollop of soured cream, if liked.

calcutta beef curry

serves 4
prep + cook time 1 hour 40 minutes + marinating time

400 g (13 oz) stewing beef, cut into bite-sized pieces
5 tablespoons natural yogurt
1 tablespoon medium curry powder
2 tablespoons mustard oil
1 dried bay leaf
1 cinnamon stick
3 cloves
4 green cardamom pods, bruised
1 large onion, halved and thinly sliced
3 garlic cloves, crushed
1 teaspoon finely grated fresh root ginger
1 teaspoon ground turmeric
1 teaspoon hot chilli powder
2 teaspoons ground cumin
400 ml (14 fl oz) beef stock
salt

1 Place the meat in a non-metallic bowl. Mix together the yogurt and curry powder and pour over the meat. Season with salt, cover and marinate in the refrigerator for 24 hours.

2 Heat the oil in a large nonstick wok or frying pan and add the spices. Stir-fry for 1 minute and then add the onion. Stir-fry over a medium heat for 4–5 minutes, then add the garlic, ginger, turmeric, chilli powder and cumin. Add the marinated meat and stir-fry for 10–15 minutes over a low heat.

3 Pour in the beef stock and bring to the boil. Reduce the heat to low, cover tightly and simmer gently, stirring occasionally, for 1 hour or until the meat is tender. Check the seasoning, remove from the heat and serve immediately with rice, if liked.

salmon fillets with sage & quinoa

serves 4
prep + cook time 20 minutes

200 g (7 oz) quinoa
100 g (3½ oz) butter, at room
    temperature
8 sage leaves, chopped
small bunch of chives
grated rind and juice of 1 lemon
4 salmon fillets, about 175 g (6 oz)
    each
1 tablespoon olive oil
salt and pepper

1 Cook the quinoa in a pan of unsalted boiling water for about 15 minutes or according to the packet instructions until cooked but firm.
2 Meanwhile, mix together the butter, sage, chives and lemon rind in a small bowl and season to taste with salt and pepper.
3 Rub the salmon fillets with the oil, season with pepper and cook in a preheated frying pan, turning carefully once, for about 8–10 minutes or until cooked through and the salmon flakes easily. Remove from the pan and leave to rest.
4 Drain the quinoa, stir in the lemon juice and season to taste. Spoon on to serving plates and top with the salmon, topping each piece with a knob of sage butter.

mackerel with avocado salsa

serves 4
prep + cook time 16–18 minutes

8 mackerel fillets
2 lemons, plus extra wedges to serve
salt and pepper

for the avocado salsa
2 ripe avocados, peeled, stoned and
    finely diced
juice and rind of 1 lime
1 red onion, finely chopped
½ cucumber, finely diced
1 handful of coriander leaves, finely
    chopped

1 Make 3 diagonal slashes across each mackerel fillet on the skin side and season well with salt and pepper. Cut the lemons in half, then squeeze the juice over the fish.
2 Lay on a grill rack, skin side up, and cook under a preheated grill for 6–8 minutes or until the skin is lightly charred and the flesh is just cooked through.
3 Meanwhile, to make the salsa, mix together the avocados and lime juice and rind, then add the onion, cucumber and coriander. Toss well to mix and season to taste with salt and pepper.
4 Serve the mackerel hot with the avocado salsa and lemon wedges for squeezing over.

Tip
Rich and creamy, avocados are brimming with almost 20 nutrients, including vitamin E, potassium, folic acid and dietary fibre, to protect against a variety of illnesses.

feta-stuffed plaice

serves 4
prep + cook time 1 hour

2 tablespoons chopped oregano
25 g (1 oz) Parma ham, finely
    chopped
2 garlic cloves, finely chopped
4 spring onions, finely chopped
200 g (7 oz) feta cheese
8 plaice fillets, skinned
300 g (10 oz) courgettes, sliced
4 tablespoons garlic-infused olive oil
8 flat mushrooms
150 g (5 oz) baby plum tomatoes,
    halved
1 tablespoon capers, rinsed and
    drained
salt and pepper

1 Put the mint, oregano, ham, garlic and spring onions in a bowl. Crumble in the feta cheese, season with plenty of pepper and mix together well.

2 Put the fish fillets, skin side up, on a clean work surface and press the feta mixture down the centres. Roll up loosely and secure with wooden cocktail sticks.

3 Scatter the courgettes into a shallow, ovenproof dish and drizzle with 1 tablespoon of the oil. Place in a preheated oven, 190°C (375°F), Gas Mark 5, for 15 minutes. Add the plaice fillets to the dish. Tuck the mushrooms, tomatoes and capers around the fish and season lightly with salt and pepper. Drizzle with the remaining oil.

4 Return to the oven for a further 25 minutes or until the fish is cooked through.

Tip
Despite its impressive appearance, this supper dish doesn't take a lot of preparation and will give all the family some brain-boosting protein.

pork & red pepper chilli

serves 4
prep + cook time 40 minutes

2 tablespoons olive oil
1 large onion, chopped
1 red pepper, cored, deseeded and
  diced
2 garlic cloves, crushed
450 g (14½ oz) minced pork
1 fresh red chilli, deseeded and finely
  chopped
1 teaspoon dried oregano
500 g (1 lb) passata
400 g (13 oz) can red kidney beans,
  drained and rinsed
salt and pepper

to garnish
soured cream
basil leaves

1 Heat the oil in a saucepan over a medium heat. Add the onion and red pepper and cook for 5 minutes until soft and starting to brown, then add the garlic and cook for another 30 seconds or so. Next, add the minced pork and cook, stirring and breaking up the meat with a wooden spoon, for 5 minutes or until browned.
2 Add the remaining ingredients, except the soured cream, and bring to the boil. Reduce the heat and simmer gently for 20 minutes. Remove from the heat, season well with salt and pepper and garnish with soured cream and basil leaves.

For lamb & aubergine chilli, replace the red pepper with 1 medium aubergine, cut into small cubes, and replace the pork with minced lamb. Sprinkle the finished dish with 2 tablespoons chopped mint leaves.

sausages & lentils in tomato sauce

serves 4
prep + cook time 1 hour 20 minutes

3 tablespoons olive oil, plus extra
   for drizzling
8 Italian pork sausages
1 onion, roughly chopped
1 celery stick, roughly chopped
3 garlic cloves, crushed
200 ml (7 fl oz) full-bodied red wine
400 g (13 oz) can chopped tomatoes
1.2 litres (2 pints) chicken stock
1 bay leaf
1 dried red chilli
125 g (4 oz) green lentils
salt and pepper

1 Heat the oil in a large, heavy-based saucepan in which the sausages fit in a single layer. Add the sausages and cook over a medium heat for 10–12 minutes until golden brown all over. Remove and set aside.

2 Add the onion and celery to the pan and cook over a low heat for 8–10 minutes until softened. Stir in the garlic and cook for a further 2 minutes.

3 Increase the heat to high, pour in the wine and boil vigorously for 2 minutes, scraping any sediment from the base of the pan. Stir in the tomatoes, stock, bay leaf and chilli and bring to the boil. Add the lentils and return the sausages to the pan. Simmer gently for 40 minutes, or until the sausages and lentils are cooked through. Season with salt and pepper. Serve with a drizzle of olive oil.

pumpkin & goats' cheese bake

serves 4
prep + cook time 45–50 minutes

400 g (13 oz) raw beetroot, peeled
    and diced
625 g (1¼ lb) pumpkin or butternut
    squash, peeled, deseeded and cut
    into slightly larger dice than the
    beetroot
1 red onion, cut into wedges
2 tablespoons olive oil
2 teaspoons fennel seeds
2 small goats' cheeses, 100 g
    (3½ oz) each
salt and pepper
chopped rosemary, to garnish

1 Put the vegetables into a roasting tin, drizzle with the oil and
sprinkle with the fennel seeds and salt and pepper. Roast in a
preheated oven, 200°C (400°F), Gas Mark 6, for 20–25 minutes,
turning once, until well browned and tender.
2 Cut the goats' cheeses into thirds and nestle among the roasted
vegetables. Sprinkle the cheeses with a little salt and pepper and
drizzle with some of the pan juices.
3 Return the dish to the oven and cook for about 5 minutes until the
cheese is just beginning to melt. Sprinkle with rosemary and serve
immediately.

spiced cabbage & bacon pan-fry

serves 2
prep + cook time 20 minutes

2 tablespoons olive oil
100 g (3½ oz) thick bacon rashers,
    cut into 1 cm (½ inch) strips
1 small onion, finely sliced
2 garlic cloves, chopped
pinch of ground allspice
pinch of ground cinnamon
¼ teaspoon grated nutmeg
½ small head Savoy cabbage, thinly
    shredded
200 g (7 oz) cauliflower florets
salt and pepper
2 tablespoons chopped parsley,
    to garnish

1 Heat the oil in a large frying pan and cook the bacon for 2–3 minutes over a medium-high heat, until golden. Add the onion and garlic and cook for a further 3–4 minutes, until beginning to soften.
2 Stir in the spices until aromatic, then add the cabbage and cauliflower and stir-fry for 7–8 minutes, until slightly softened but still with some bite. Season to taste, garnish with parsley, then heap into deep bowls to serve.

Tip
This winter warmer takes just 20 minutes to prepare, so a bowlful is a great choice for a fast midweek supper in front of the fire.

quinoa-stuffed tomatoes with mozzarella

serves 4
prep + cook time 30 minutes

400 ml (14 fl oz) vegetable stock
200 g (7 oz) quinoa, rinsed under
    running water
1 tablespoon extra virgin rapeseed
    oil
200 g (7 oz) chestnut mushrooms,
    chopped
2 small courgettes, diced
2 spring onions, finely chopped
2 tablespoons toasted sunflower
    seeds
1 small bunch of chopped basil
finely grated zest of 1 lemon
8 small or 4 large tomatoes
125 g (4 oz) mozzarella, sliced
salt and pepper

1 Pour the vegetable stock into a medium-sized saucepan and bring to the boil. Tip the quinoa into the pan, cover and simmer gently for 12–15 minutes. It is ready when the seed begins to come away from the germ. Remove from the heat and drain off any stock that hasn't been absorbed.

2 Meanwhile, preheat the oven to 200°C (400°F), Gas Mark 6 and heat the oil in a large frying pan over a medium heat. Add the mushrooms and cook, stirring, for 4–5 minutes, then add the courgettes. Cook for a further 4–5 minutes, then stir in the spring onions, sunflower seeds, basil, lemon rind and cooked quinoa and season well with salt and pepper.

3 Cut the tops off the tomatoes and scoop out the seeds. Spoon the quinoa mixture into the tomatoes, then top each tomato with the sliced mozzarella. Place on a lightly greased baking tray. Replace the lids, then bake in the oven for 15–18 minutes until the mozzarella melts. Serve with crisp salad leaves, if liked.

goats' cheese & butternut squash stuffed peppers

serves 2
prep + cook time 30 minutes

2 tablespoons olive oil
2 red peppers, halved, cored and
 deseeded
175 g (6 oz) butternut squash,
 peeled, deseeded and cut into
 small chunks
1 small red onion, roughly chopped
2 tablespoons black olive tapenade
75 g (3 oz) soft goats' cheese,
 crumbled
2 tablespoons fresh breadcrumbs
1 tablespoon grated Parmesan
 cheese

1 Heat 1 tablespoon of the oil in a large frying pan, add the peppers, cut side down, and cook for 2 minutes, then turn the peppers over and cook for a further 2 minutes. Remove from the pan.
2 Meanwhile, heat the remaining oil in a separate frying pan, add the squash and onion and cook for 5 minutes until slightly softened. Remove from the pan and toss with the tapenade in a bowl, then add the goats' cheese and gently toss together.
3 Spoon the mixture into the pepper halves, then place the peppers in a roasting tin and scatter with the breadcrumbs and Parmesan.
4 Place in a preheated oven, 200°C (400°F), Gas Mark 6, for 15 minutes until the tops are golden and cooked through. Serve hot with a simple salad, if liked.

south indian vegetable stew

serves 4
prep + cook time 35–40 minutes

1 tablespoon groundnut oil
6 shallots, halved and thinly sliced
2 teaspoons black mustard seeds
8–10 curry leaves
1 fresh green chilli, thinly sliced
2 teaspoons peeled and finely grated
    fresh root ginger
1 teaspoon ground turmeric
2 teaspoons ground cumin
6 black peppercorns
2 carrots, cut into thick batons
1 courgette, cut into thick batons
200 g (7 oz) French beans, trimmed
1 potato, peeled and cut into thin
    batons
400 ml (14 fl oz) coconut milk
400 ml (14 fl oz) vegetable stock
2 tablespoons lemon juice
salt and pepper

1 Heat the oil in a large frying pan over a medium heat. Add the shallots and stir-fry for 4–5 minutes. Add the mustard seeds, curry leaves, chilli, ginger, turmeric, cumin and peppercorns, and stir-fry for a further 1–2 minutes until fragrant.

2 Add the carrots, courgette, beans and potato to the pan. Pour in the coconut milk and stock and bring to the boil. Reduce the heat to low, cover and simmer gently for 12–15 minutes until the vegetables are tender. Season to taste, remove from the heat and squeeze over the lemon juice just before serving.

For spicy tomato, vegetable & coconut curry, follow the recipe above, replacing the turmeric, cumin and peppercorns with 2 tablespoons hot curry powder, and the vegetable stock with 400 ml (14 fl oz) tomato passata.

quick one-pot ratatouille

serves 4
prep + cook time 30 minutes

100 ml (3½ fl oz) olive oil
2 onions, chopped
1 aubergine, cut into bite-sized
   cubes
2 large courgettes, cut into bite-sized
   pieces
1 red pepper, cored, deseeded and
   cut into bite-sized pieces
1 yellow pepper, cored, deseeded
   and cut into bite-sized pieces
2 garlic cloves, crushed
400 g (13 oz) can chopped tomatoes
4 tablespoons chopped parsley or
   basil
salt and pepper

1 Heat the oil in a large saucepan until very hot. Add the onions, aubergine, courgettes, red and yellow peppers and garlic, and cook, stirring constantly, for a few minutes until softened. Add the tomatoes, season with salt and pepper and stir well.

2 Reduce the heat, cover the pan tightly and simmer for 15 minutes until all the vegetables are cooked. Remove from the heat and stir in the chopped parsley or basil before serving.

lentil moussaka

serves 2
prep + cook time 55 minutes + standing time

125 g (4 oz) brown or green lentils,
    picked over, rinsed and drained
400 g (13 oz) can chopped tomatoes
2 garlic cloves, crushed
½ teaspoon dried oregano
pinch of ground nutmeg
150 ml (¼ pint) vegetable stock
2–3 tablespoons olive oil
250 g (8 oz) aubergine, sliced
1 onion, finely chopped

cheese topping
1 egg
150 g (5 oz) soft cheese
pinch of ground nutmeg
salt and pepper

1 Put the lentils in a saucepan with the tomatoes, garlic, oregano and nutmeg. Pour in the stock. Bring to the boil, then reduce the heat and simmer for 20 minutes until the lentils are tender but not mushy, topping up with extra stock as needed.

2 Meanwhile heat the oil in a frying pan and lightly fry the aubergine and onion, until the onion is soft and the aubergine is golden on both sides. Layer the aubergine mixture and lentil mixture alternately in an ovenproof dish.

3 Make the topping. In a bowl, beat together the egg, cheese and nutmeg with a good dash of salt and pepper. Pour over the moussaka and cook in a preheated oven, 200°C (400°F), Gas Mark 6, for 20–25 minutes.

4 Remove from the oven and leave to stand for 5 minutes before serving with salad leaves, if liked.

food for friends

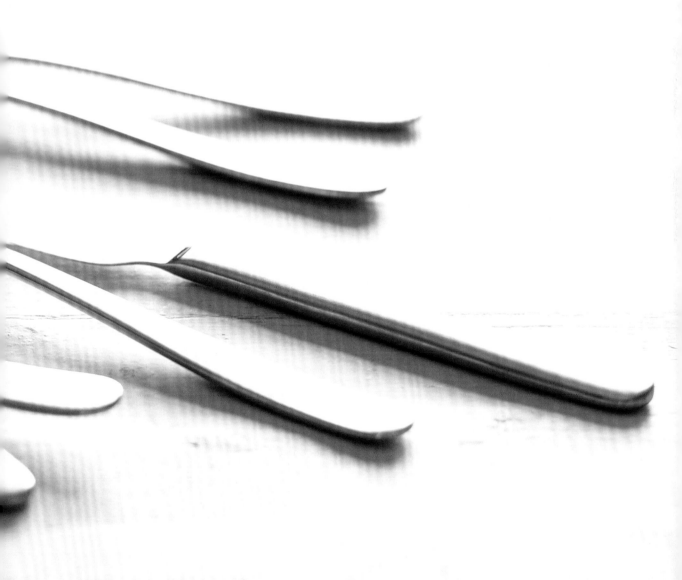

courgette frittatas with mint

serves 6
prep + cook time 40 minutes

1 tablespoon olive oil
1 onion, finely chopped
2 courgettes, about 375 g (12 oz)
 in total, halved lengthways and
 thinly sliced
6 eggs
300 ml (½ pint) milk
3 tablespoons grated Parmesan
 cheese
2 tablespoons chopped mint, plus
 extra leaves to garnish (optional)
salt and pepper

tomato sauce
1 tablespoon olive oil
1 onion, finely chopped
1–2 garlic cloves, crushed
 (optional)
500 g (1 lb) plum tomatoes,
 chopped

1 Make the sauce. Heat the oil in a saucepan, stir in the onion and fry for 5 minutes, stirring occasionally until softened and just beginning to brown. Add the garlic, if using, the tomatoes and season with salt and pepper. Stir and simmer for 5 minutes until the tomatoes are soft. Purée in a liquidizer or food processor until smooth, sieve into a bowl and keep warm.

2 Heat the oil in a frying pan, add the onion and fry until softened and just beginning to brown. Add the courgettes, stir to combine and cook for 3–4 minutes until softened but not browned.

3 Beat together the eggs, milk, Parmesan and mint, then stir in the courgettes. Season well and pour the mixture in the 12 greased sections of a deep muffin tin. Bake into a preheated oven, 190°C (375°F), Gas Mark 5, for about 15 minutes until they are lightly browned and well risen and the egg mixture has set.

4 Leave in the tin for 1–2 minutes, then loosen the edges with a knife. Turn out and arrange on plates with the warm tomato sauce. Garnish with extra mint leaves, if liked.

goats' cheese & chive soufflés

serves 6
prep + cook time 30–35 minutes

25 g (1 oz) unsalted butter
2 tablespoons plain flour
250 ml (8 fl oz) milk
100 g (3½ oz) soft goats' cheese
3 eggs, separated
2 tablespoons chopped chives
salt and pepper

1 Melt the butter in a saucepan, add the flour and cook over a low heat, stirring, for 30 seconds.
2 Remove the pan from the heat and gradually stir in the milk until smooth. Return to the heat and cook, stirring constantly, until the mixture thickens. Cook for 1 minute.
3 Leave to cool slightly, then beat in the goats' cheese, egg yolks, chives, and salt and pepper to taste.
4 Whisk the egg whites in a large, perfectly clean bowl, until soft peaks form. Fold the egg whites into the cheese mixture. Spoon the mixture into 4 greased, individual soufflé ramekins and set on a baking sheet. Bake in a preheated oven, 200°C (400°F), Gas Mark 6, for 15–18 minutes until risen and golden. Serve immediately.

For cheddar & chilli soufflés, replace the goats' cheese with grated Cheddar and the chives with finely chopped coriander leaves. Beat 2 finely chopped deseeded red chillies, according to taste, into the egg yolk mixture.

coconut spiced clams

serves 4
prep + cook time 20 minutes

4 tablespoons vegetable oil
2 shallots, very finely chopped
1 red chilli, slit lengthways and
   deseeded
3 cm (1 inch) piece of fresh root
   ginger, peeled and shredded
2 garlic cloves, finely chopped
2 plum tomatoes, finely chopped
1 tablespoon medium or hot curry
   powder
200 ml (7 fl oz) canned coconut
   milk
800 g (1¾ lb) fresh clams,
   scrubbed (see tip)
1 large handful of chopped
   coriander leaves
3 tablespoons grated fresh
   coconut
salad
crusty bread

1 Heat the oil in a large wok or saucepan until hot, add the shallots, red chilli, ginger and garlic and stir-fry over a medium heat for 3–4 minutes. Increase the heat to high, stir in the tomatoes, curry powder and coconut milk and cook for a further 4–5 minutes.

2 Add the clams to the pan, discarding any that have cracked or don't shut when tapped, stir to mix and cover tightly, then continue to cook over a high heat for 6–8 minutes until the clams have opened. Discard any that remain closed.

3 Stir in the chopped coriander and sprinkle over the grated coconut. Ladle into bowls and serve immediately with a fresh salad and crusty bread to mop up the juices.

Tip
To clean fresh clams,
soak them in fresh water
for 20 minutes, then scrub
the outsides with a
stiff brush.

harissa salmon with spicy sweet potato

serves 4

prep + cook time 45–50 minutes + marinating time

2 tablespoons natural yogurt
2 teaspoons harissa
2 tablespoons chopped coriander, plus extra to garnish
grated rind and juice of ½ lime
4 pieces of skinless salmon fillet, about 150 g (5 oz) each
vegetable oil, for oiling
lime wedges and flat-leaf parsley, to serve

spicy sweet potato
500 g (1 lb) sweet potato, peeled and cut into chunks
1 tablespoon olive oil
1 teaspoon cumin seeds
½ teaspoon garam masala
salt and black pepper

1 Mix together the yogurt, harissa, coriander and lime rind and juice in a non-metallic bowl. Add the salmon and coat in the mixture. Cover and marinate in the refrigerator for at least 20 minutes.

2 Toss together the sweet potato chunks, olive oil, cumin seeds and garam masala in a bowl and season well. Put in a roasting tin and place in a preheated oven, 200°C (400°F), Gas Mark 6, for 35–40 minutes until golden.

3 Heat a lightly oiled frying pan or griddle until hot towards the end of the sweet potato roasting time. Add the salmon and cook for 3 minutes on each side until just cooked. Garnish with coriander and serve with the sweet potatoes, lime wedges and flat-leaf parsley.

For spicy chicken drumsticks, make the marinade as above and stir in 1 teaspoon groundnut oil. Score 8 chicken drumsticks, cover with the marinade and marinate as above. Place under a hot grill for 12–15 minutes until cooked through.

roast garlic-studded monkfish

serves 4
prep + cook time 50 minutes +
marinating time

1 kg (2 lb) monkfish tail, trimmed
 and boned
3–4 bay leaves
1 teaspoon fennel seeds
4 garlic cloves, cut into thick
 slivers
4 tablespoons olive oil
a few thyme sprigs
2 red peppers, cored, deseeded
 and roughly chopped
1 aubergine, cut into bite-sized
 chunks
2 courgettes, cut into bite-sized
 chunks
3 ripe plum tomatoes, cut into
 chunks
3 tablespoons lemon juice
salt and pepper

to garnish
2 tablespoons salted capers,
 rinsed and chopped
3 tablespoons chopped flat leaf
 parsley

1 Lay the bay leaves over one monkfish fillet and scatter over the fennel seeds. Lay the other fillet on top and tie at 2.5 cm (1 inch) intervals with fine string. With the tip of a sharp knife, make slits all over the fish and push in the garlic slivers. Put the oil, thyme and a little pepper into a glass dish, add the monkfish and turn to coat well. Cover and marinate in the refrigerator for at least 2 hours or overnight.
2 Remove from the marinade. Pour 2 tablespoons of the marinade into a heavy, nonstick frying pan and heat until almost smoking. Add the monkfish and cook, turning, for 2–3 minutes until sealed. Set aside.
3 Heat the remaining marinade in the pan. Add the vegetables and quickly brown. Transfer to a heavy, shallow baking dish, set the monkfish on top and add the tomatoes and lemon juice. Bake in a preheated oven, 220°C (425°F), Gas Mark 7, for 20 minutes, basting and turning the vegetables occasionally.
4 Remove the string and cut the fish into thick slices. Season the vegetables with salt and pepper. Serve the monkfish on the vegetables, garnished with the capers and parsley.

sri lankan scallop curry

serves 4
prep + cook time 30–35 minutes

1 tablespoon groundnut oil
¼ teaspoon turmeric
1 teaspoon cumin seeds
2 fresh red chillies, deseeded and
    chopped
1 onion, finely chopped
6 tomatoes, peeled, deseeded and
    diced
3 tablespoons medium curry
    powder
1 tablespoon coconut cream
1 teaspoon ground cumin
1 teaspoon garam masala
400 g (13 oz) fresh king scallops
small handful of finely chopped
    coriander leaves
salt and pepper

1 Heat the oil in a frying pan over a low heat. Add the turmeric, cumin seeds and chillies, and fry briefly to release the flavours. Add the onion and cook gently for 10 minutes until softened but not coloured.

2 Stir in the tomatoes and curry powder and simmer for 5 minutes or until the tomatoes have cooked down to a thick sauce. Stir in the coconut cream, ground cumin and garam masala and season to taste.

3 Add the scallops and cook for a few minutes until the scallops are just cooked through. Check the seasoning and adjust if necessary. Stir in the coriander and serve immediately.

vegetable broth & sea bass

serves 4
prep + cook time 12–13 minutes

750 ml (1¼ pints) chicken or
vegetable stock
1 fennel bulb, cut into 8 wedges,
herby tops reserved (optional)
12 fine asparagus spears
150 g (5 oz) frozen peas, thawed
150 g (5 oz) broad beans, podded
2 tablespoons olive oil
4 sea bass fillets, about 200 g
(7 oz) each, skin on and
pin-boned (see tip)
small handful of mint leaves, torn
small handful of basil leaves, torn
salt and pepper

1 Put the stock in a large saucepan and bring to the boil. Add the fennel, reduce the heat and simmer for 3 minutes or until almost tender. Add the asparagus, peas and broad beans and cook for a 1–2 minutes. Season with salt and pepper.

2 Meanwhile, heat the oil in a frying pan over a medium heat. Season the sea bass with salt and pepper and place, skin side down, in the pan. Cook for 3–4 minutes or until the skin is crispy, then turn the fish over and cook for a further minute.

3 Ladle the vegetable broth into bowls and sprinkle with a few torn mint and basil leaves. Top the broth with the pan-fried sea bass and reserved herby fennel tops, if liked, and serve.

Tip
Pin bones are the tiny bones just below the surface of the fish. Ask your fishmonger to pin-bone the sea bass fillets for you.

baked lemon sole & asparagus

serves 2
prep + cook time 30 minutes

15 g (½ oz) unsalted butter,
   softened
1 tablespoon chopped herbs, such
   as parsley, thyme and chives
4 skinned lemon sole fillets
4 spring onions, shredded
1 carrot, cut into matchsticks
1 tablespoon white wine
finely grated rind of ½ lemon
salt and pepper

pan-fried asparagus
15 g (½ oz) unsalted butter
1–2 teaspoons olive oil
125 g (4 oz) asparagus spears

1 Mix together the butter and herbs and spread on to one side of each of the sole fillets. Roll up the fish with the herb butter on the inside.

2 Cut 4 squares of baking parchment, each about 25 x 25 cm (10 x 10 inches). Put the spring onions and carrot in the centre of 2 of the pieces of parchment and top each with 2 of the sole rolls. Drizzle over the wine and sprinkle over the lemon rind. Season with salt and pepper. Put the other pieces of baking parchment on top and tightly roll up each side to make 2 parcels.

3 Transfer the parcels to a baking sheet and bake in a preheated oven, 200°C (400°F), Gas Mark 6, for about 20 minutes.

4 Meanwhile, cook the asparagus. Heat the butter and oil in a frying pan. Add the asparagus and fry for 2–3 minutes until just tender. Season to taste. Arrange the asparagus on serving plates and scatter over some Parmesan shavings. Add the fish parcels and serve.

roasted trout with rocket pesto

serves 4
prep + cook time 50–55 minutes

400 g (13 oz) can haricot beans,
    drained
250 g (8 oz) cherry tomatoes,
    halved
1 red onion, chopped
4 fresh trout, heads removed
salt and pepper

rocket pesto
50 g (2 oz) rocket, plus extra to
    garnish
25 g (1 oz) pine nuts
40 g (1½ oz) Parmesan cheese,
    finely grated
8 tablespoons olive oil

1 Tip the beans into a large roasting tin, add the cherry tomatoes, onion and some seasoning and mix together. Slash each side of the trout two or three times with a knife. Tuck the bean mixture in between the slits.

2 To make the pesto, finely chop the rocket leaves and pine nuts and pound in a pestle and mortar. Alternatively, blitz in a blender or food processor. Mix with the Parmesan, oil and some seasoning. Spoon a little of the pesto into the cuts in the trout and the inside of the fish, then spoon the rest of the mixture into a small bowl. Cover the bowl and chill until required.

3 Roast the trout in a preheated oven, 190°C (375°F), Gas Mark 5, for 20–25 minutes depending on their size. Test by pressing a knife into the centre of the trout through the body cavity: if the fish flakes evenly and is an even colour it is ready. Transfer to serving plates and serve with spoonfuls of pesto and extra rocket, if liked.

For basil pesto,
process 50 g (2 oz) basil,
1 crushed garlic clove,
4 tablespoons pine nuts,
100 ml (3½ fl oz) olive oil
until smooth. Stir in
2 tablespoons grated
Parmesan.

plaice with applewood crust

serves 4
prep + cook time 22–24 minutes

4 x 150 g (5 oz) plaice fillets
75 g (3 oz) dry white breadcrumbs
3 tablespoons chopped flat-leaf
   parsley
1 garlic clove, crushed
finely grated rind of ½ lemon
25 g (1 oz) walnuts, finely chopped
25 g (1 oz) Applewood or
   Lancashire cheese, finely grated
2 tablespoons seasoned flour
1 egg, beaten
25 g (1 oz) butter
1 tablespoon olive oil
salt and pepper

1 Place half the breadcrumbs in a blender or food processor with the chopped parsley and garlic and blend together until the breadcrumbs are slightly green. Mix these breadcrumbs into the remaining crumbs, together with the lemon rind, walnuts and cheese. Season with salt and pepper and mix together well.

2 Sprinkle a little seasoned flour over each plaice fillet, then dip the flesh side of each fillet into the beaten egg. Place the fillets, skin side down, on a baking sheet and sprinkle the breadcrumb mixture over the fish. Melt the butter with the olive oil and drizzle over the top.

3 Cook the fish on the top shelf of a preheated oven, 200°C (400°F), Gas Mark 6, for 12–14 minutes, or until the crust is golden brown and the fish cooked through. Serve with wedges of lemon, fresh herbs, matchstick chips and a green salad.

spring braised duck

serves 4
prep + cook time 2 hours 5 minutes

4 duck legs
2 teaspoons plain flour
25 g (1 oz) butter
1 tablespoon olive oil
2 onions, sliced
2 streaky bacon rashers, finely
    chopped
2 garlic cloves, crushed
1 glass white wine, about 150 ml
    (¼ pint)
300 ml (½ pint) chicken stock
3 bay leaves
500 g (1 lb) small new potatoes
200 g (7 oz) fresh peas
150 g (5 oz) asparagus tips
2 tablespoons chopped mint
salt and pepper

1 Halve the duck legs through the joints. Mix the flour with a little seasoning and use to coat the duck pieces.
2 Melt the butter with the oil in a sturdy roasting pan or flameproof casserole and gently fry the duck pieces for about 10 minutes until browned. Drain to a plate and pour off all but 1 tablespoon of the fat left in the pan.
3 Add the onions and bacon to the pan and fry gently for 5 minutes. Add the garlic and fry for a further 1 minute. Add the wine, stock and bay leaves and bring to the boil, stirring. Return the duck pieces and cover with a lid or foil. Place in a preheated oven, 160°C (325°F), Gas Mark 3, for 45 minutes.
4 Add the potatoes to the pan, stirring them into the juices. Sprinkle with salt and return to the oven for 30 minutes.
5 Add the peas, asparagus and mint to the pan and return to the oven for a further 15 minutes or until all the vegetables are tender. Check the seasoning and serve.

For spring braised chicken, replace the duck with 4 chicken thighs and omit the bacon. Add 200 g (7 oz) baby turnips, 100 g (3½ oz) baby carrots, 2 small, sliced courgettes along with the peas and asparagus. Cook as above.

teriyaki chicken with three seeds

serves 4
prep + cook time 36–40 minutes
+ marinating time

4 boneless, skinless chicken
  breasts, about 125 g (4 oz) each
2 tablespoons sunflower oil
4 tablespoons soy sauce
2 garlic cloves, finely chopped
2.5 cm (1 inch) piece root ginger,
  finely grated
2 tablespoons sesame seeds
2 tablespoons sunflower seeds
2 tablespoons pumpkin seeds
juice of 2 limes
100 g (3½ oz) herb salad
½ small iceberg lettuce, torn into
  bite-sized pieces
50 g (2 oz) alfalfa or brocco
  sprouting seeds

1 Put the chicken breasts into a shallow china dish. Spoon three-quarters of the oil over the chicken, then add half the soy sauce, the garlic and the ginger.
2 Turn the chicken to coat in the mixture, then leave to marinate for 30 minutes.
3 Heat a nonstick frying pan, then lift the chicken out of the marinade and add to the pan. Fry for 8–10 minutes each side until dark brown and cooked all the way through. Lift out and set aside.
4 Heat the remaining oil in the pan, add the seeds and fry for 2–3 minutes until lightly toasted. Add the remaining marinade and remaining soy sauce, bring to the boil, then take off the heat and mix in the lime juice.
5 Mix the herb salad, lettuce and sprouting seeds together, then spoon over 4 serving plates. Thinly slice the chicken and arrange on top, then spoon the seed and lime dressing over the top. Serve at once.

chicken with 30 garlic cloves

serves 4

prep + cook time 1 hour 55 minutes

4 chicken leg and thigh joints
25 g (1 oz) butter
1 tablespoon olive oil
250 g (8 oz) shallots, halved if large
2 tablespoons plain flour
200 ml (7 fl oz) dry white wine
200 ml (7 fl oz) chicken stock
2 teaspoons Dijon mustard
3 garlic bulbs
small bunch thyme
4 tablespoons crème frâiche,
  optional
salt and pepper

1 Fry the chicken in the butter and oil in a frying pan, until golden on both sides. Transfer to a large casserole dish.

2 Fry the shallots until softened and lightly browned. Stir in the flour, then gradually mix in the wine, stock, mustard and seasoning. Bring to the boil, stirring.

3 Separate the garlic cloves but do not peel them. Count out 30 cloves and add to the casserole dish with 3–4 thyme stems. Pour over the wine mix, then cover and cook in a preheated oven, 180°C (350°F), Gas Mark 4, for 1½ hours.

4 Stir in the crème fraiche, if using, and serve with mashed potato or sweet potato and green beans, if liked.

chicken with spring vegetables

serves 4
prep + cook time 1 hour 25 minutes
+ resting time

1.5 kg (3 lb) chicken
about 1.5 litres (2½ pints) hot
    chicken stock
2 shallots, halved
2 garlic cloves
2 sprigs of parsley
2 sprigs of marjoram
2 sprigs of lemon thyme
2 carrots, halved
1 leek, trimmed and sliced
200 g (7 oz) tenderstem broccoli
250 g (8 oz) asparagus, trimmed
½ Savoy cabbage, shredded

1 Put the chicken in a large saucepan and pour over enough stock just to cover the chicken. Push the shallots, garlic, herbs, carrots and leek into the pan and place over a medium-high heat. Bring to the boil, then reduce the heat and simmer gently for 1 hour or until the chicken is falling away from the bones.
2 Add the remaining vegetables to the pan and simmer for a further 6–8 minutes or until the vegetables are cooked.
3 Turn off the heat and leave to rest for 5–10 minutes before serving the chicken and vegetables in deep bowls with spoonfuls of the broth. Remove the skin, if preferred, and serve with plenty of crusty bread.

Tip
This is a super-easy dish to prepare for friends, as it needs very little attention and cooks away gently so you can get on with preparing the rest of the meal.

beef with walnut pesto

serves 4
prep + cook time 2 hours + resting time

150 g (5 oz) walnut pieces
2 garlic cloves, roughly chopped
50 g (2 oz) can anchovies
2 tablespoons hot horseradish
   sauce
25 g (1 oz) chopped parsley
2 tablespoons olive oil
1.5 kg (3 lb) rolled topside or top
   rump of beef
1 large onion, finely chopped
2 celery sticks, chopped
300 ml (½ pint) red wine
150 ml (¼ pint) beef stock
4 carrots, cut into chunky slices
300 g (10 oz) baby turnips
500 g (1 lb) new potatoes
200 g (7 oz) French beans
salt and pepper
chopped parsley, to garnish

1 Put the walnuts in a food processor or blender with the garlic, anchovies and their oil, horseradish, parsley, 1 tablespoon of the oil and plenty of pepper and blend to a thick paste, scraping the mixture down from the sides of the bowl.

2 Untie the beef and open it out slightly. If there is already a split through the flesh, make the cut deeper so that it will take the stuffing. If it is a perfectly rounded piece of beef, make a deep cut so that you can pack in the stuffing. Once the stuffing is in place, reshape the meat into a roll. Tie with string, securing at 2.5 cm (1 inch) intervals. Pat the meat dry with kitchen paper and season with salt and pepper.

3 Heat the remaining oil in a flameproof casserole and fry the meat on all sides to brown. Drain to a plate.

4 Add the onion and celery to the pan and fry gently for 5 minutes. Return the meat to the pan and pour the wine and stock over it. Add the carrots and turnips. Bring just to the boil, cover with a lid and place in a preheated oven, 160°C (325°F), Gas Mark 3. Cook for 30 minutes.

5 Tuck the potatoes around the beef and sprinkle with salt. Return to the oven for a further 40 minutes until the potatoes are tender. Stir in the beans and return to the oven for 20 minutes until the beans have softened. Leave to rest for 15 minutes before carving the meat.

For beef with hazelnut pesto, omit the walnuts and use the same quantity of hazelnuts. Replace the anchovies with 4 tablespoons capers and the turnips with the same quantity of swede, cut into chunks.

loin of pork with lentils

serves 5–6
prep + cook time 2 hours
10 minutes + resting time

175 g (6 oz) Puy lentils
875 g (1¾ lb) pork loin, rind
    removed, boned and rolled
2 tablespoons olive oil
2 large onions, sliced
3 garlic cloves, sliced
1 tablespoon finely chopped
    rosemary
300 ml (½ pint) chicken or
    vegetable stock
250 g (8 oz) baby carrots,
    scrubbed and left whole
salt and pepper

1 Put the lentils in a saucepan, cover with water and bring to the boil. Boil rapidly for 10 minutes, then drain well.

2 Sprinkle the pork with salt and pepper. Heat the oil in a large heavy-based frying pan and brown the meat on all sides. Transfer to a casserole dish and add the lentils.

3 Add the onions to the pan and fry for 5 minutes. Stir in the garlic, rosemary and stock and bring to the boil. Pour over the meat and lentils and cover with a lid. Place in a preheated oven, 180°C (350°F), Gas Mark 4, for 1 hour.

4 Stir the carrots into the casserole, season well and return to the oven for a further 20–30 minutes until the pork is cooked through and the lentils are soft. Drain the meat, transfer to a serving platter and leave to rest in a warm place for 20 minutes. Carve into thin slices, then serve with the lentils, carrots and juices.

pork fillet with mushrooms

serves 4
prep + cook time 30–37 minutes

4 tablespoons olive oil
500 g (1 lb) pork tenderloin, sliced
　　into 5 mm (¼ inch) discs
300 g (10 oz) mushrooms, trimmed
　　and cut into chunks
1 lemon
300 ml (½ pint) crème fraîche
2 sprigs of tarragon, leaves
　　stripped
salt and pepper

1 Heat 2 tablespoons of the oil in the pan over a medium-high heat and fry the pork slices for 3–4 minutes, turning once so that they are browned on both sides. Remove with a slotted spoon.
2 Add the remaining oil to the pan, tip in the mushrooms and cook for 3–4 minutes, stirring occasionally, until softened and golden.
3 Cut half of the lemon into slices and add to the pan to brown a little on each side, then remove and set aside.
4 Return the pork to the pan, add the crème fraîche and tarragon and pour in the juice from the remaining lemon. Season well, bring to the boil, then reduce the heat and leave to bubble gently for 5 minutes. Add the prepared lemon slices at the last minute and gently stir through.
5 Serve the pork wih quinoa, brown rice or the potato puffs below.

For potato puffs, cut 1 kg (2 lb) new potatoes in half and lay them, cut-side up, in an ovenproof dish. Season and roast (without any oil) in a preheated oven, 220°C (425°F), Gas Mark 7, for 30–35 minutes until cooked through and puffed up.

malaysian rendang lamb

serves 4
prep + cook time 3 hours

2 tablespoons sunflower oil
1 kg (2 lb) leg of lamb, butterflied
2 onions, finely chopped
1 tablespoon ground coriander
1 teaspoon ground turmeric
6 garlic cloves, crushed
6 tablespoons very finely chopped
    lemon grass
4–6 bird's eye chillies, chopped
4 tablespoons finely chopped
    fresh coriander root and stem
400 ml (14 fl oz) coconut milk
salt and pepper

1 Heat the oil in a deep, heavy-based casserole dish and brown the lamb on both sides for about 5–6 minutes.

2 Place the remaining ingredients in a food processor and blend until smooth. Season well.

3 Pour this mixture over the lamb and bring to the boil. Cover tightly and cook in a preheated oven at 150°C (300°F), Gas Mark 2, turning the lamb occasionally, for 2½ hours or until the lamb is meltingly tender and most of the liquid has evaporated.

4 Remove from the oven and allow to stand for 10–12 minutes before serving, cut into thick slices.

For cucumber & mint raita, as an accompaniment, mix 175 ml (6 fl oz) natural yogurt with 75 g (3 oz) deseeded, grated cucumber, 2 tablespoons chopped mint, a pinch ground cumin, lemon juice and salt to taste.

index

almonds
   broccoli & almond soup 34
   roasted almonds with paprika 19
anchovies: butter bean & anchovy
   pâté 16
asparagus
   asparagus, tomato & feta frittata 62
   baked lemon sole & asparagus 112
aubergine
   lamb & aubergine chilli 92
   quick one-pot ratatouille 100
avocado
   chilled avocado soup 32
   guacamole with vegetable dippers
      21
   mackerel with avocado salsa 89
   smoked mackerel salad with
      orange & avocado 45
   spicy quinoa, broad bean &
      avocado salad 51

bacon
   corn & bacon muffins 25
   rosemary, bacon & brie muffins 24
   soft boiled egg & bacon salad 54
   spiced cabbage & bacon pan-fry
      95
   sweet potato, bacon & cabbage
      soup 40
baked cabbage with nuts & cheese 70
baked chillies with cheese 19
baked lemon sole & asparagus 112
baked sweet potatoes 63
barley: chicken & barley risotto 82
beans
   broad bean & mint hummus with
      wholegrain crostini 17
   butter bean & anchovy pâté 16
   spicy quinoa, broad bean &
      avocado salad 51
   squash, kale & mixed bean soup
      38
beef
   beef with hazelnut pesto 121
   beef with walnut pesto 121
   calcutta beef curry 86
   peppered beef with salad leaves 71
beetroot: parsnip & beetroot crisps
   with dukkah 22
broad bean & mint hummus with
   wholegrain crostini 17
broccoli
   broccoli & almond soup 34
   broccoli & stilton soup 34
   squash & broccoli soup 40
buckwheat & salmon salad 47
bulgar wheat: warm chicken, veg &
   bulgar salad 56

butter bean & anchovy pâté 16
butternut squash see squash

cabbage
   baked cabbage with nuts & cheese
      70
   spiced cabbage & bacon pan-fry
      95
   sweet potato, bacon & cabbage
      soup 40
cajun-spiced turkey meatballs 85
calcutta beef curry 86
carrots: warm scallop, parsnip & carrot
   salad 43
cheddar & chilli soufflés 105
cheese
   asparagus, tomato & feta frittata 62
   baked cabbage with nuts & cheese
      70
   baked chillies with cheese 19
   broccoli & stilton soup 34
   cheddar & chilli soufflés 105
   cheese & chive mayonnaise 23
   cheesy croutons 41
   feta-stuffed plaice 90
   feta, herb & rocket frittata 66
   goats' cheese & butternut squash
      stuffed peppers 97
   goats' cheese & chive soufflés 105
   lentil & feta salad 46
   mushrooms with camembert on
      toast 60
   plaice with applewood crust 115
   pumpkin & goats' cheese bake 94
   quinoa-stuffed tomatoes with
      mozzarella 96
   ricotta-stuffed mushrooms 66
   root vegetable bake with nuts &
      cheese 70
   rosemary, bacon & brie muffins 24
   stilton welsh rarebit 66
   wholemeal cheese straws 26
chicken
   chicken & barley risotto 82
   chicken skewers with spiced
      chickpea mash 73
   chicken with 30 garlic cloves 118
   chicken with spring vegetables 119
   gingered chicken, seed & vegetable
      rice 78
   green chicken kebabs 83
   smoked chicken salad 55
   spicy chicken drumsticks 108
   spinach & chicken curry 80
   spring braised chicken 116
   teriyaki chicken with three seeds
      117
   thai chicken curry 81

   warm chicken, veg & bulgar salad
      56
chickpeas
   chicken skewers with spiced
      chickpea mash 73
   lamb, chickpea & cinnamon broth
      39
chilled avocado soup 32
chillies
   baked chillies with cheese 19
   cheddar & chilli soufflés 105
   lamb & aubergine chilli 92
   pork & red pepper chilli 92
citrus olives 19
clams, coconut spiced 106
coconut
   coconut spiced clams 106
   lime & coconut squid salad 42
   spicy tomato, vegetable & coconut
      curry 99
cod: green cod steaks 83
corn
   corn & bacon muffins 25
   spiced corn & spring onion muffins
      25
courgettes
   courgette & dill soup 35
   courgette frittatas with mint 104
   quick one-pot ratatouille 100
   quinoa, courgette & pomegranate
      salad 48
   spiced courgette fritters 65
crispy sweet potato skins 63
crostini
   broad bean & mint hummus with
      wholegrain crostini 17
   smoked mackerel crostini 14
crunchy vegetable salad 53
cucumber & mint raita 124
curries
   calcutta beef curry 86
   south indian vegetable stew 99
   spicy tomato, vegetable & coconut
      curry 99
   spinach & chicken curry 80
   sri lankan scallop curry 110
   thai chicken curry 81

duck: spring braised duck 116
dukkah: parsnip & beetroot crisps with
   dukkah 22

eggs
   asparagus, tomato & feta frittata 62
   cheddar & chilli soufflés 105
   courgette frittatas with mint 104
   feta, herb & rocket frittata 66
   goats' cheese & chive soufflés 105

greek-style summer omelette 74
moroccan baked eggs 75
pea & leek omelette 68
soft boiled egg & bacon salad 54

fennel: pink grapefruit & fennel salad 52
feta-stuffed plaice 90
feta, herb & rocket frittata 66
fish & seafood
  baked lemon sole & asparagus 112
  buckwheat & salmon salad 47
  butter bean & anchovy pâté 16
  coconut spiced clams 106
  feta-stuffed plaice 90
  green cod steaks 83
  harissa salmon with spicy sweet potato 108
  lime & coconut squid salad 42
  mackerel with avocado salsa 89
  plaice with applewood crust 115
  roast garlic-studded monkfish 109
  roasted trout with rocket pesto 114
  salmon fillets with sage & quinoa 88
  smoked mackerel crostini 14
  smoked mackerel salad with orange & avocado 45
  spiced tuna open sandwiches 66
  sri lankan scallop curry 110
  vegetable broth & sea bass 111
  warm scallop, parsnip & carrot salad 43
frittata
  asparagus, tomato & feta frittata 62
  courgette frittatas with mint 104
  feta, herb & rocket frittata 66
fritters, spiced courgette 65

garlic
  chicken with 30 garlic cloves 118
  garlic mushrooms on sourdough toast 60
  roast garlic-studded monkfish 109
gingered chicken, seed & vegetable rice 78
goats' cheese & butternut squash stuffed peppers 97
goats' cheese & chive soufflés 105
grapefruit: pink grapefruit & fennel salad 52
greek salad 74
greek-style summer omelette 74
green chicken kebabs 83
green cod steaks 83
guacamole with vegetable dippers 21

haloumi with paprika oil 19
harissa salmon with spicy sweet potato 108
herbed soda breads 27
hummus: broad bean & mint hummus with wholegrain crostini 17

kale: squash, kale & mixed bean soup 38
kebabs, green chicken 83

lamb
  lamb & aubergine chilli 92
  lamb, chickpea & cinnamon broth 39
  malaysian rendang lamb 124
leeks: pea & leek omelette 68
lemon sole: baked lemon sole & asparagus 112
lentils
  lentil & feta salad 46
  lentil moussaka 101
  loin of pork with lentils 122
  sausages & lentils in tomato sauce 93
  spinach & red lentil soup 37
lime & coconut squid salad 42
loin of pork with lentils 122

mackerel
  mackerel with avocado salsa 89
  smoked mackerel crostini 14
  smoked mackerel salad with orange & avocado 45
malaysian rendang lamb 124
mayonnaise
  cheese & chive 23
  parsley 23
meatballs, cajun-spiced turkey 85
mint
  broad bean & mint hummus with wholegrain crostini 17
  courgette frittatas with mint 104
  cucumber & mint raita 124
monkfish: roast garlic-studded monkfish 109
moroccan baked eggs 75
moussaka, lentil 101
muffins
  corn & bacon 25
  rosemary, bacon & brie 24
  spiced corn & spring onion 25
mushrooms
  garlic mushrooms on sourdough toast 60
  mushrooms with camembert on toast 60
  pork fillet with mushrooms 123
  ricotta-stuffed mushrooms 66

nuts
  baked cabbage with nuts & cheese 70
  beef with hazelnut pesto 121
  beef with walnut pesto 121
  broccoli & almond soup 34
  roasted almonds with paprika 19
  root vegetable bake with nuts & cheese 70

oatcakes: rosemary oatcakes 29
olives, citrus 19
omelettes
  greek-style summer 74
  pea & leek 68
orange: smoked mackerel salad with orange & avocado 45

parsnips
  parsnip & beetroot crisps with dukkah 22
  root chips with parsley mayonnaise 23
  warm scallop, parsnip & carrot salad 43
pâté, butter bean & anchovy 16
pea & leek omelette 68
peppered beef with salad leaves 71
peppers
  goats' cheese & butternut squash stuffed peppers 97
  pork & red pepper chilli 92
pesto
  basil 114
  hazelnut 121
  rocket 114
  walnut 121
pink grapefruit & fennel salad 52
plaice
  feta-stuffed plaice 90
  plaice with applewood crust 115
pomegranate: quinoa, courgette & pomegranate salad 48
pork
  loin of pork with lentils 122
  pork & red pepper chilli 92
  pork fillet with mushrooms 123
potatoes
  potato puffs 123
  root chips with parsley mayonnaise 23
pumpkin
  pumpkin & goats' cheese bake 94
  squash & pumpkin seed salad 49

quick one-pot ratatouille 100
quinoa
  quinoa-stuffed tomatoes with mozzarella 96
  quinoa, courgette & pomegranate salad 48
  salmon fillets with sage & quinoa 88
  spicy quinoa, broad bean & avocado salad 51

raita
  cucumber & mint 124
  spicy 65
ratatouille, quick one-pot 100
rice
  chicken & barley risotto 82

gingered chicken, seed & vegetable rice 78
ricotta-stuffed mushrooms 66
risotto, chicken & barley 82
roast garlic-studded monkfish 109
roasted almonds with paprika 19
roasted trout with rocket pesto 114
root chips with parsley mayonnaise 23
root vegetable bake with nuts & cheese 70
rosemary oatcakes 29
rosemary, bacon & brie muffins 24

salads
  buckwheat & salmon 47
  crunchy vegetable 53
  greek 74
  lentil & feta 46
  lime & coconut squid 42
  pink grapefruit & fennel 52
  quinoa, courgette & pomegranate 48
  smoked chicken 55
  smoked mackerel salad with orange & avocado 45
  soft boiled egg & bacon 54
  spicy quinoa, broad bean & avocado 51
  squash & pumpkin seed 49
  warm chicken, veg & bulgar 56
  warm scallop, parsnip & carrot 43
salmon
  buckwheat & salmon salad 47
  harissa salmon with spicy sweet potato 108
  salmon fillets with sage & quinoa 88
sausages & lentils in tomato sauce 93
scallops
  sri lankan scallop curry 110
  warm scallop, parsnip & carrot salad 43
sea bass: vegetable broth & sea bass 111
seafood *see* fish & seafood
smoked chicken salad 55
smoked mackerel crostini 14

smoked mackerel salad with orange & avocado 45
soft boiled egg & bacon salad 54
soufflés
  cheddar & chilli 105
  goats' cheese & chive 105
soups
  broccoli & almond 34
  broccoli & stilton 34
  chilled avocado 32
  courgette & dill 35
  lamb, chickpea & cinnamon broth 39
  spinach & red lentil 37
  squash & broccoli 40
  squash, kale & mixed bean 38
  summer vegetable 41
  sweet potato, bacon & cabbage 40
south indian vegetable stew 99
spiced cabbage & bacon pan-fry 95
spiced corn & spring onion muffins 25
spiced courgette fritters 65
spiced tuna open sandwiches 66
spicy chicken drumsticks 108
spicy quinoa, broad bean & avocado salad 51
spicy tomato, vegetable & coconut curry 99
spinach
  spinach & chicken curry 80
  spinach & red lentil soup 37
spring braised chicken 116
spring braised duck 116
squash
  goats' cheese & butternut squash stuffed peppers 97
  squash & broccoli soup 40
  squash & pumpkin seed salad 49
  squash, kale & mixed bean soup 38
squid: lime & coconut squid salad 42
sri lankan scallop curry 110
stilton welsh rarebit 66
summer vegetable soup 41
sweet potatoes
  baked sweet potatoes 63
  crispy sweet potato skins 63

harissa salmon with spicy sweet potato 108
root chips with parsley mayonnaise 23
sweet potato, bacon & cabbage soup 40

tapas 19
teriyaki chicken with three seeds 117
thai chicken curry 81
tomatoes
  asparagus, tomato & feta frittata 62
  quinoa-stuffed tomatoes with mozzarella 96
  sausages & lentils in tomato sauce 93
  spicy tomato, vegetable & coconut curry 99
trout: roasted trout with rocket pesto 114
tuna: spiced tuna open sandwiches 66
turkey: cajun-spiced turkey meatballs 85

vegetables (mixed)
  chicken with spring vegetables 119
  crunchy vegetable salad 53
  gingered chicken, seed & vegetable rice 78
  guacamole with vegetable dippers 21
  root vegetable bake with nuts & cheese 70
  south indian vegetable stew 99
  spicy tomato, vegetable & coconut curry 99
  summer vegetable soup 41
  vegetable broth & sea bass 111
  warm chicken, veg & bulgar salad 56

warm chicken, veg & bulgar salad 56
warm scallop, parsnip & carrot salad 43
welsh rarebit, stilton 66
wholemeal cheese straws 26

Acknowledgements

Special photography: © Octopus Publishing Group Limited
Stephen Conroy 27, 42, 55, 64, 67 top right, 69, 71, 87, 88, 89, 92, 93, 100, 101, 105, 109, 113, 119, 123, 125
Will Heap 22, 24, 36, 39, 41, 44, 48, 52, 74, 80, 81, 84, 95, 98, 110
William Lingwood 16 19, top right
David Munns 82, 117, 118
Lis Parsons 17,19 bottom left, 21, 23, 26, 28, 43, 46, 47, 49, 53, 56, 57, 67 top left and bottom left, 70, 72, 75, 79, 91, 96, 97, 116
Craig Robertson 25, 50, 107
William Shaw 15, 19 top left and bottom right, 33, 34, 35, 38, 40, 67 bottom right, 83, 94, 104, 108, 114, 115
Ian Wallace 61, 62, 63

Other photography: Han V Vonno/Thinkstock 1; Svetl/Thinkstock 2–3

BUILT FOR SUCCESS

THE STORY OF

McDonald's

First published in the UK in 2011 by
Franklin Watts
338 Euston Road
London NW1 3BH

Franklin Watts Australia
Level 17/207 Kent Street
Sydney, NSW 2000

First published by Creative Education, an imprint of The
Creative Company.

A CIP catalogue record for this book is available from the
British Library.

ISBN: 978 1 4451 0596 3

Dewey number: 338.7'6164795

Printed in China

Franklin Watts is a division of
Hachette Children's Books,
an Hachette UK company.

www.hachette.co.uk

DESIGN AND PRODUCTION BY **ZENO DESIGN**

PHOTOGRAPHS BY Alamy (Ferruccio, Kevin Foy, Jeff
Greenberg, Kim Karpeles, Oleksiy Maksmenko, Jiri Rezac,
Helene Rogers, Stephen Saks Photography, Vario Images
GmbH & Co.KG, Jim West), Corbis (Louie Psihoyos), Getty
Images (Tim Boyle, Focus on Sport, LUI JIN/AFP, Guang
Niu, Thos Robinson, Art Shay//Time Life Pictures, Brendan
Smialowski, Mario Tama)

BUILT FOR SUCCESS

THE STORY OF

McDonald's

W
FRANKLIN WATTS
LONDON • SYDNEY

SARA GILBERT

On 15 April 1955, the first McDonald's franchise restaurant opened in Des Plaines, Illinois, USA, with cheeseburgers, French fries (chips) and milkshakes on the menu and cheerful men and women serving food from behind a counter. Fifty years later, on 15 April 2005, another new restaurant opened just a few kilometres away in Chicago – a 2,230 square metre (24,000 sq ft) McDonald's, built to commemorate the iconic restaurant's 50th anniversary. The new McDonald's was fitted with 18 metre (60 foot) Golden Arches, double drive-through lanes and seating for 300 – a far cry from the original drive-in. But despite the physical differences, the commitment to quality and customer service that had started half a century earlier was the same as ever.

CHAPTER ONE

Beginning with burgers

It was milkshakes, not hamburgers, that lured Ray Kroc to San Bernardino, California, in 1954. Restaurateurs Dick and Mac McDonald were operating eight multi-mixer machines, which were used to make milkshakes in their drive-in and Kroc, who sold the machines, was eager to learn why. So he flew from his home in Chicago to California to see the McDonald's restaurant for himself.

Kroc was surprised to see a queue of cars and people form outside the service window at lunch. When he asked one of the men in the queue what the attraction was, the customer said, "You'll get the best hamburger you ever ate for 15 cents [10p]." Kroc quizzed the other people waiting and learned that many of them came for a lunch of burgers, chips and milkshakes every day. He was so impressed that the next day, in a meeting with the McDonald brothers, he suggested they franchise their Speedee Service System, which allowed them to make their limited menu quickly using an efficient kitchen setup, in restaurants across the country.

The brothers, who had already licenced the concept to a handful of other restaurants in the western USA, were wary of attempting to franchise their **fast-food** restaurant

McDonald's original Speedee Service System logo promised inexpensive hamburgers served quickly on a large scale. They didn't want the burden of regulating the restaurants but Kroc volunteered to handle that for them.

With the hesitant blessing of the McDonald brothers, Kroc formed a franchising company – originally known as McDonald's System Inc – on 2 March 1955 in Oak Brook, Illinois. His original intent was to establish franchises of the McDonald's restaurant to drive sales of the multi-mixer machines he sold. And although his sole source of income until 1961 would be the £7,500 ($12,000) salary he earned from selling multi-mixers (he had decided not to take wages from McDonald's until the business had turned a profit), it quickly became clear that 10p (15-cent) burgers, not milkshakes, would be the base of his business.

Kroc opened his first McDonald's in Des Plaines, Illinois, in April 1955, often helping to sweep floors and clean toilets himself to get the business off the ground, and to establish what would become the operating principle for the company: "Quality, Service, Cleanliness and Value". Fred Turner, who would later become president and eventually chairman of the company, was one of the first grill cooks at the restaurant. He later recalled seeing his boss walk around picking up every bit of McDonald's litter he found. "He'd come into the store with both hands full of cups and wrappers," Turner said. "He was the store's outside pick-up man."

Kroc was also busy finding franchisees to open more McDonald's. In his first year, the company built 18 restaurants, almost half of them in California. When it became clear that trying to maintain uniform standards at restaurants 3,218 kilometres (2,000 miles) away was nearly impossible, Kroc decided to focus his efforts closer to Chicago. His first real taste of success came in Waukegan, Illinois, where a franchise opened on 26 May 1955. On its first day, the restaurant almost ran out of bread rolls before 5.00pm and sold £280 ($450) worth of food; the following day sales nearly doubled and queues stretched down the road. By day three, the restaurant cleared £625 ($1,000) in sales.

McDonald's® SYSTEM

MAY I HAVE YOUR ORDER PLEASE?
MAY I HELP YOU M'AM (SIR)?

	HAMBURGERS Per Dozen		
	CHEESEBURGERS Per Dozen	.15 ea. 1.80	
	FRENCH FRIES	.19 ea. 2.28	
	MILK-SHAKES ☐ Chocolate ☐ Strawberry ☐ Vanilla	.10 ea. .20 ea.	
	COKE Extra Large		
	ORANGE Extra Large	.10 ea. .15 ea.	
	ROOT BEER Extra Large	.10 ea. .15 ea.	
	MILK	.10 ea. .15 ea.	
	COFFEE ☐ Cream ☐ Black	.10 ea.	

Soon the owners of the Waukegan franchise were making more money than Kroc. But he had achieved something far more significant than dollars – he had found success. That was enough to help convince other prospective franchisees that opening a McDonald's was a worthwhile venture. By 1958, a total of 34 restaurants were open; in 1959, 67 more were added. By the company's fifth anniversary in 1960, McDonald's had 200 franchisees operating in almost a dozen US states with total annual sales of £23 million ($37 million).

But Kroc was still struggling to turn a profit. The terms of his contract with the McDonald brothers dictated that his company receive only 1.9 per cent of each franchisee's food sales – and a quarter of that went back to the brothers. The one-time franchise fee was only £590 ($950) per shop. As a result the money Kroc brought in was barely enough to cover the expense of helping the individual shop managers get started and to pay the wages of the growing **executive** team.

It was the ingenuity of one of those executives, Harry Sonneborn, that turned the tide for McDonald's. In 1957, he set up Franchise Realty Corporation to locate and **lease** sites for shops, then sublet the properties to the franchisees with a mark-up based on a formula related to volume of sales. The plan provided an immediate **revenue** stream for the company and gave Kroc more control over the franchisees and where they could be located.

The company had to go into **debt** to fund the rapid growth that would allow it to start profiting from its property programme. The best way to maximise the business's money, Kroc believed, was to purchase the rights to the McDonald's trade name and fast-food system outright from Mac and Dick McDonald, which would eliminate the percentage of sales going directly to them. The brothers asked for £1.7 million ($2.7 million), which was much more than Kroc had available. But he and Sonneborn found **lenders**, obtained the necessary funds and, in 1961, bought out the brothers. Kroc believed he would get the better deal in the long term.

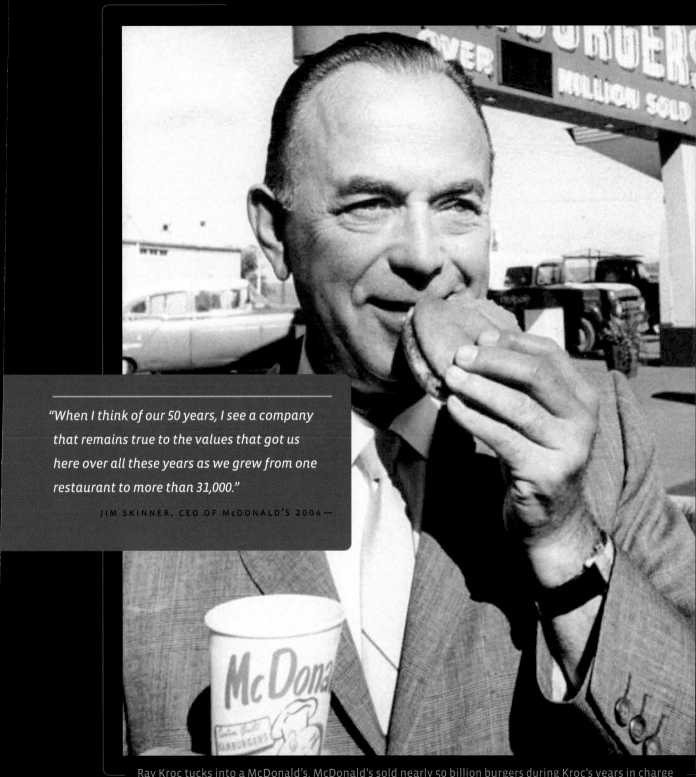

"When I think of our 50 years, I see a company that remains true to the values that got us here over all these years as we grew from one restaurant to more than 31,000."

JIM SKINNER, CEO OF McDONALD'S 2004—

Ray Kroc tucks into a McDonald's. McDonald's sold nearly 50 billion burgers during Kroc's years in charge

THE ORIGINAL ARCHES

When architect Stanley Meston agreed to design a building for the McDonald brothers' new restaurant in 1952, he had no idea that it would become an icon of American popular culture. He also had no idea that the very element he refused to incorporate would become its most recognisable feature. But when Dick McDonald presented him with sketches that incorporated two towering arches on either side of the building, Meston stoutly refused to add them, saying that if the arches stayed, he would go. To appease Meston McDonald told him to leave them out. But after Meston finished his drawings, McDonald took them to a sign maker and asked him to add the arches. The sign maker added decorative bright yellow arches which could be seen down the road and were the most prominent part of the building. "The arches were the whole thing," McDonald said. "Without them, it was just another rectangular building."

CHAPTER TWO

McDonald's on the map

Buying out the McDonald brothers was the start of a new era for Ray Kroc and his company. Now he was free to implement his own ideas and to control the growing network of fast-food franchises as he saw fit. He was very keen on uniformity amongst all of his restaurants and insisted on a commitment to quality, cleanliness and superb customer service from each one.

That quality control became even more important as the franchise started expanding at an increasingly rapid rate in the 1960s, adding more than 500 locations over the course of the decade.

Marketing the restaurants became just as important. In its early days, McDonald's had invested almost nothing in national advertising, although it encouraged its franchisees to advertise locally. Its first national ad was a one-page advertisement in *Reader's Digest* in 1963, the same year that the company produced its first two television spots. In 1964, McDonald's would retain a national ad agency. By 1967, it would establish its own internal marketing department. Soon its inventive **jingles**, including the memorable "You Deserve a Break Today" slogan, and its jovial mascot, a clown called Ronald McDonald, would be broadcast widely over television and radio airwaves.

This museum exhibit captures the romanticism of the 1960s, a decade of rapid growth for McDonald's

But McDonald's emerging dominance was based on far more than catchy slogans and colourful clowns. In 1963, McDonald's celebrated two milestones – opening its 500th restaurant and selling its one billionth hamburger. Sales were climbing and Kroc was taking home a handsome annual salary of about £71, 645 ($115,000). But to really maximise the company's potential he and the other principal owners of the company – Sonneborn, who had been named chief executive officer (CEO) in 1960, and June Martino, Kroc's longtime secretary – knew they would have to take McDonald's public to raise capital to help the company grow.

On 15 April 1965 – a decade after Kroc's first restaurant opened – McDonald's became a publicly owned company with an **initial public offering** (IPO) of stock to investors at £14 ($22.50) a share. Although **brokers** on New York City's Wall Street, where much of the nation's stocks are traded, were wary of a business many of them had not heard of (McDonald's had not yet broken into the New York market) investors across the country were intrigued by the opportunity. By the end of the first day of trading, the price for a share had shot up to £18.70 ($30); within a week, it had climbed to £22.50 ($36). Suddenly the owners of McDonald's were millionaires.

That financial boost from the stock offering loosened the purse strings at McDonald's Corporation, as the company had been renamed. Sonneborn paid £46,725 ($75,000) for a three-and-a-half minute television spot during the 1965 Macy's Thanksgiving Day Parade (a traditional parade to mark the US Thanksgiving holiday). He even agreed to **sponsor** a secondary school marching brass band that wore McDonald's Golden Arches on its uniforms. The investment paid off: during the month following the parade sales increased nationwide by eight per cent.

The payoff from the parade advertising led to another landmark decision. In 1966, McDonald's was approached by the CBS television network about advertising during a new sporting event: the first Super Bowl, an American

"McDonald's and the city of Chicago have really grown together. On behalf of Chicago, thanks to McDonald's for 50 great years of service to customers, not only in Chicago but around the globe."

RICHARD M DALEY, MAYOR OF CHICAGO

From TV adverts to giant balloons, McDonald's has long played a part in the Macy's Thanksgiving Day Parade in New York

football championship game. Sonneborn bargained the £124,600 ($200,000) asking price down to £105, 900 ($170,000) and purchased a similar spot on the NBC network, which was also televising the game, for £46,725 ($75,000).

It was a bit of a gamble as it was a first-time broadcast of a brand-new event but it proved to be one of the best advertising buys McDonald's ever made. A full 41 per cent of households in the USA tuned in to watch American football team the Green Bay Packers defeat the Kansas City Chiefs 35–10, making it the highest-rated programme of the year and one of the most widely watched in television history. And McDonald's, which was the only sponsor on both networks, saw an immediate boost in sales. The chain's average sales per restaurant for January 1967 jumped 22 per cent over the same month's sales the previous year.

McDonald's was also making more money because it was expanding its menu – often due to the innovative ideas of the franchisees themselves. The Filet-O-Fish sandwich was introduced in 1964, the Big Mac in 1968 and the Shamrock Shake – a minty milkshake – in the early 1970s. Kroc even tried a little product development of his own. Shortly before the Filet-O-Fish became a successful non-meat alternative he tried the Hulaburger – a slice of pineapple, topped with a slice of cheese and served on a bread roll. It was a failure.

Kroc may have struggled with new product innovation but he didn't with new restaurants. In 1968, McDonald's Corporation opened its 1,000th location; in 1970, as it sold its five billionth hamburger, McDonald's officially reached all 50 states. But in the midst of the explosive growth trouble sprouted. Kroc and his longtime right-hand man, Harry Sonneborn, had developed differing views about how quickly the company should grow. The showdown between the two men culminated in 1967 when Sonneborn resigned at Kroc's request. When the stunned **board of directors** found out they demanded to know who would be replacing him. Kroc immediately thought of Fred Turner, who at the time was the head of operations for the company. "We'll put Fred Turner in there," Kroc replied. "He's a smart guy and he can learn. He can do it."

McDonald's sponsored the first Super Bowl American football game, introducing the company to millions of viewers

THE BIRTH OF THE BIG MAC

McDonald's most famous sandwich was born in Pittsburgh, Pennsylvania, in 1967. Jim Delligatti, who operated a dozen McDonald's restaurants in the city, wanted something bigger and better on his menu. So he started stacking burgers and bread rolls together. He called his sandwich – two beef burgers separated by a centre section of roll and accompanied by lettuce, pickles, onion and a 'secret sauce' – the Big Mac. When he put it on his menu as a test it cost a whopping 30p (45 cents) – quite a jump from the standard 10p (15 cent) burgers. But hungry customers were willing to pay for the Big Mac. Within months it was being tested in more markets and by 1968, it was available at every McDonald's restaurant in the USA. "This wasn't like discovering the light bulb," Delligatti said. "The bulb was already there. All I did was screw it in the socket."

CHAPTER THREE

Franchise fever

Fred Turner officially took over as president in 1968, just as the fast-food industry in the USA was exploding. Burger King, McDonald's closest competitor, was opening up 100 shops each year. New US regional fast-food chains were being introduced, from Jack in the Box in the West to Minnie Pearl's Chicken in the South.

Dave Thomas had also just launched Wendy's fast-food restaurant chain with the intention of cutting into McDonald's **market share**. McDonald's reign as the market leader was facing its first serious threat.

Turner decided to abandon Sonneborn's earlier plan of slowing the addition of new shops. In fact he went in the opposite direction entirely. "There was pent-up consumer demand throughout the system," Turner later said. "All of our markets needed more outlets." So he doubled staff in both the property and construction departments and embarked on an aggressive growth plan. In 1969, 211 new locations opened – a number that continued increasing until 1974 when 515 more restaurants were opened. By then McDonald's had a total of 3,000 restaurants across the USA and was far and away the fast-food industry leader.

In the 1960s, Burger King became a serious rival of McDonald's and remains its chief competitor today.

McDonald's growth was fed in part by a new trend in American lifestyles. As the 1970s progressed, suburban housing developments were becoming popular. People were spending more time in their cars and wanted faster dining options. But while the other fast-food franchises were being swallowed up by corporate **conglomerates**, McDonald's had stayed true to its core business principles. As the fast-food landscape changed, the commitment to quality and customer service that had been part of the business from the beginning proved to be its greatest strength.

McDonald's annual sales surged past £625 million ($1 billion) for the first time in 1972. The opening of the first drive-through window at a restaurant in Sierra Vista, Arizona, in 1975 helped push that figure beyond £1.9 billion ($3 billion) in 1976. By then McDonald's had a total of 4,177 shops in 22 countries.

McDonald's first foray into international franchising had come in 1967 with a restaurant in British Columbia in Canada and another in Puerto Rico. The international market became a major source of growth in the 1970s, as the possibility for expansion within the US market began to diminish. Although Kroc had floated a number of ideas in the 1960s and 1970s for diversifying the business, from a Disney-like theme park in California to a German-themed restaurant in Chicago, none of them had seemed like good investments of the company's cash. Instead McDonald's focused on expanding beyond the USA's borders for growth.

At the time, few other American food businesses had ventured much further than Canada for expansion. Boldly, McDonald's sought to establish franchises in Europe and Asia, where fast food in general and hamburgers in particular were still unknown, in an effort to reach new markets. The first McDonald's in the UK opened in London in 1974. It was the 3,000th McDonald's branch and, after a shaky start, became a big hit.

But there was still work to be done at home in the USA as well. As McDonald's place in society grew, its menu had to grow with it. The launch of a breakfast line,

for example, began with the Egg McMuffin – an idea that started at a restaurant in California and was introduced throughout the McDonald's system in 1973. The sandwich was made with eggs fried on the grill in non-stick muffin rings, then topped with a grilled rasher of bacon.

In 1979, the company started selling Happy Meals as an occasional promotional product. While the idea was more about packaging than a new product, it had an immediate impact on sales. Originally hamburgers, chips and a soft drink were served in collectible boxes designed as circus train carriages; children could collect the whole set during a designated time frame. Happy Meals (which now usually include a small toy or prize) soon became so popular that they earned a place on the menu all year round.

The development of one of McDonald's most popular menu items – chicken nuggets – came in response to changing American tastes. As the 1980s began, people were choosing to eat less beef and Kroc wanted to introduce a chicken main course. He even hired a chef, Rene Arend, to help. But Arend's early efforts – a deep fried chicken pie, for example – weren't working either. It was when Arend took a break from chicken and started experimenting with 'Onion Nuggets' – bite-sized chunks of battered and fried onions – that Turner, by then CEO, took note. "Why not try chicken nuggets instead?" he suggested.

By 1983, the nuggets were ready to roll out; by 1985, McNuggets accounted for more than £436 million ($700 million) of McDonald's approximately £7 billion ($11 billion) in sales and McDonald's had become the second-largest chicken retailer in the fast-food industry, just behind Kentucky Fried Chicken. But Ray Kroc, long known as the hamburger king, wasn't around to compare sales figures with Colonel Sanders, the chicken king. Late in 1983, the founder of the McDonald's franchise suffered a series of strokes and was hospitalised. Although he had worked full-time until then, he never returned to his office again. In January 1984, aged 82, Ray Kroc died.

McDonald's Happy Meals packaging and toys often tie in with popular children's films of the time

IN 1955 RAY A. KRO

McDONALD'S SYSTEM WITH THE HIGH

QUALITY, SERVICE, CLEANLINESS, AND

PERSISTENCE, AND LEADERSHIP HAVE GUI

OUR LOCATION IN DES PLAINES, ILLINOIS T

THE KROC FILES

More than half of Ray Kroc's life was over by the time he discovered McDonald's in 1954. He'd already been trained as a World War One ambulance driver for the Red Cross (working with cartoon pioneer Walt Disney), a piano player, a paper cup salesman and a dancer by the time his job selling multi-mixer milkshake machines took him to the McDonald's drive-in in San Bernardino, California, in 1954. But spreading the McDonald's concept across the country became his life's work. "I was 52 years old," he said. "I had diabetes and incipient arthritis. I had lost my gall bladder and most of my thyroid gland in earlier campaigns, but I was convinced that the best was ahead of me." Kroc, who was born in Oak Park, Illinois, in 1902 and died in 1984, devoted the final 30 years of his life to building McDonald's into the largest restaurant company in the world.

CHAPTER FOUR

Changing of the McGuard

McDonald's celebrated its 30th birthday in 1985 having surpassed Ray Kroc's wildest dreams. Sales had exceeded £6.25 billion ($10 billion). More than 50 billion hamburgers had been sold at approximately 8,300 restaurants in 36 countries.

The company continued in growth mode: on average a new McDonald's restaurant opened somewhere in the world every 17 hours. By 1988, there would be more than 10,000 McDonald's operating globally.

Much of that development flourished under new leadership. Michael Quinlan, who had started working at the company in 1963 as a part-time post-room clerk, took over as president in 1982 and succeeded Turner as CEO in 1987. In his first year as CEO Quinlan opened 600 new restaurants around the world, laying the groundwork for unprecedented expansion by the company. Quinlan was so aggressive that, at one point in the 1980s, McDonald's was opening five restaurants a day, adamantly defying the notion that the fast-food market was saturated, or filled to capacity. "Saturation applies to our competitors, not to us," Quinlan confidently told shareholders in 1989.

Within a decade Quinlan's efforts had introduced McDonald's to a total of 106 countries and had more than doubled company sales. When the first McDonald's

As America filled with McDonald's restaurants in the 1980s, the company looked to global markets

opened in Moscow in 1990, more than 30,000 people waited in the cold to visit the restaurant; two years later, an opening in Beijing attracted 40,000 customers on the first day. Queues at restaurants in Poland and Israel made news as well. With a network of more than 22,000 restaurants worldwide, by 1997, McDonald's had displaced Coca-Cola as the world's best-known **brand**, according to Interbrand, a London-based consulting firm.

But amidst such international acclaim the brand was becoming beleaguered at home. For one thing franchisees were growing concerned that the rapid rate of growth – which often placed new restaurants within the same neighbourhood as existing locations – would cut into their sales. With fast-food restaurants now quite common in the USA domestic sales were levelling off by the mid-1990s.

Another problem was that public perception of the restaurants was shifting. As more people became aware of the importance of healthy food choices, consumers were increasingly concerned that the food served at McDonald's, including deep-fried items and those made from animal products, was laden with fat, salt and cholesterol. More consumers also became worried about the impact that McDonald's packaging products – many of which were made of polystyrene – had on the environment.

The company's efforts to address those problems were only partially successful. While salads had been added to the menu in 1987, further attempts to diversify the chain's menu didn't go over as well. McDonald's tried fried chicken, pasta, Mexican fajitas and pizza, but none caught on with customers. Even the McLean Deluxe, a 91 per cent fat-free beef burger that was introduced in 1991 in response to health concerns, died out, remaining on the menu for only five years before disappearing.

While tinkering with the menu didn't solve the issue of McDonald's food being unhealthy, the company's efforts to soften its impact on the environment were more successful. In 1990, the company made a commitment to spend at least £62.5 million ($100 million) annually on recycled products, from table

tops to toilet rolls. The company also worked with the US Environmental Defense Fund to develop a comprehensive solid waste reduction programme; switching to paper wrappers for burgers, which had previously been served in plastic containers, resulted in a 90 per cent reduction in waste from wrapping materials. "McDonald's is proving that a company can do well by doing good," said Fred Krupp, the executive director of the Environmental Defense Fund.

Yet even amidst such improvements consumers were drifting away from McDonald's and towards competitors such as Wendy's and Burger King, which had launched the Big King burger to compete with the Big Mac. It soon became apparent to McDonald's management team that the company could not sustain such explosive growth, at least not within the USA. After opening 1,130 restaurants domestically in 1995, it scaled back to 400 additions in 1997. In addition, plans to open hundreds of smaller units in Wal-Mart shops and petrol stations were shelved because test sites weren't meeting their goals.

In the wake of taste tests which showed consumers preferred the taste of burgers from other restaurants, McDonald's also decided to go back to the kitchen to rethink some of its food production. The resulting Arch Deluxe, a 'quarter-pound' (115g) burger served with bacon, lettuce, tomato and a 'secret' mustard sauce, was introduced in 1996. While McDonald's marketed the burger and its companion sandwiches – the Fish Filet Deluxe, Grilled Chicken Deluxe and Crispy Chicken Deluxe – as 'grown-up' options, the new line failed miserably. They were priced too high – £1.40–£1.9 ($2.25–$3.00) – and had too many calories, consumers said. And the expensive marketing campaign, which featured kids and even a gregarious Ronald McDonald, put off many people.

In mid-1998, Quinlan resigned as CEO and was replaced by Jack Greenberg, the head of American business operations for McDonald's. Quinlan, who stayed on as chairman of the company, said it was time for a change. "I think it's time to utilise the tremendous depth of management skills at McDonald's as we move into the next century," he said.

> "If I were going to live to be a hundred, I'd be down here [in the offices] every day of the week."
>
> RAY KROC

While McDonald's has tried many menu items, hamburgers remain at the heart of its business

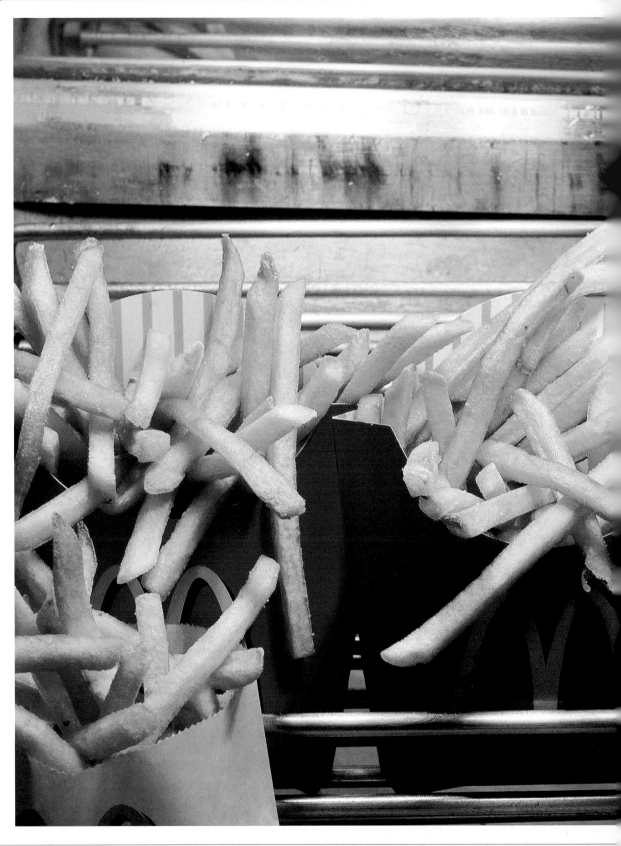

McDONALD'S WEIGHT PROBLEM

In the summer of 2002, two overweight teenagers from New York City filed a class-action, or group, lawsuit against McDonald's. The girls, both of whom ate at the restaurant frequently, claimed that the Big Macs, Egg McMuffins and Happy Meals that they consumed had made them obese and unhealthy. They contended that McDonald's had not adequately disclosed the amount of fat, sugar, salt and cholesterol in its food. A judge twice dismissed the case, saying that McDonald's could not be blamed by consumers who chose to eat its food and that its advertising was not deceptive. "We trusted that common sense would prevail in the case, and it did," McDonald's spokesperson Lisa Howard said. "McDonald's food can fit into a healthy, well-balanced diet based upon the choice and variety available on our menu." The lawsuit was revived in appeals court in January 2005; in October 2010, the case was again dismissed by the judge.

CHAPTER FIVE

Trying for a turnaround

Greenberg joined a relatively new crew of McDonald's executives when he took over as CEO. McDonald's had long been known for shepherding executives from its own grills to the corporate suites but now, hearing from both Wall Street and its own franchisees that its business strategies were stale, the company decided to look for help from the outside.

A former executive from the Long John Silver's seafood company had already been chosen to overhaul menu planning and a former leader from Pizza Hut was brought in to lead the American sales force. A month after Greenberg was installed as CEO he announced that, for the first time in its 43-year history, McDonald's Corporation would have to make redundancies. About 525 jobs at corporate headquarters – almost a quarter of the staff – were slashed. That led to another first since the company had gone public in 1965 – **net income** dropped from £1 billion ($1.64 billion) in 1997 to £940 million ($1.5 billion) in 1998.

It was apparent that McDonald's could no longer rely on burgers alone to make money. A series of **acquisitions**, beginning in 1998 with the purchase of a minority stake in the Colorado-based Chipotle Mexican Grill chain and culminating in the purchase of a 33% stake in the US arm of the UK sandwich restaurant chain Pret a Manger in 2001, were intended to diversify the company's holdings.

Jack Greenberg tried to expand McDonald's business holdings after taking over as CEO in 1998

But while the company looked elsewhere for growth its burger business was suffering. Sales were so sluggish that, in 2002, the company announced another round of redundancies, as well as the closure of almost 200 restaurants, mostly in the USA. Franchisees were frustrated by the costly new 'Made for You' production system, which was introduced in 1998 to help make McDonald's foods fresher for each customer but resulted in increasing service times instead. Consumers were also rebelling against the high fat content in many items on McDonald's menu; the issue would be made even larger with the 2004 release of *Super Size Me*, a documentary film that showed the health problems of a man who ate nothing but McDonald's food for an entire month.

By the end of 2002, McDonald's network of almost 30,000 restaurants worldwide was struggling. The stock price had dropped by 60 per cent in the course of three years; debt was adding up while profits were declining. By late December 2002, the board of directors asked Greenberg to leave and enticed former president Jim Cantalupo out of retirement to return as CEO.

Cantalupo created a new plan that called for a dramatic decrease in new locations and for the closure of more than 700 shops that were failing. He put the company's partner brands – including Chipotle – on hold and scrapped a costly £625 million ($1 billion) technology project that would have changed the computer systems in all the restaurants. He started thinking about how to update the brand image to attract teenagers and young adults once again. Then he asked an old friend, Fred Turner, to come back to the company and help McDonald's refocus on its food and its service. Cantalupo introduced his new 'Plan to Win' to the company's 1.6 million employees by saying, "I offer no false promises, no silver bullets. However, under my leadership neither failure nor second place is an option."

By the end of 2003, Cantalupo's efforts were achieving results. Sales were up, including a dramatic increase at locations that had been open a year or more, and customers were coming back for burgers – now generally priced

Film maker Morgan Spurlock attacked the high fat content of McDonald's menu in his documentary *Super Size Me*.

at around 60p ($1), thanks in part to the new 'I'm Lovin' It' ad campaign, which featured everyday people from around the world singing a catchy jingle about their affection for McDonald's. As the 60-year-old CEO prepared for the annual meeting of McDonald's restaurant owners in Orlando, Florida, he was over the moon. "Does it get any better than this?" he asked Mike Roberts, head of US operations at the time. But Cantalupo would not find out. The next day, he suffered a heart attack and died.

The turnaround that Cantalupo had set in motion, however, continued under his successor, Jim Skinner. By the time it celebrated its 50th birthday in 2005, McDonald's was reporting improved **cash flow**, higher profits and continued growth around the world.

McDonald's fortunes continued to rise. By the end of 2006, as restaurants instituted longer hours and added premium products from salads to snack wraps to their menus, McDonald's share price had risen by 25 per cent. While the company remained cautious of rapid expansion it built hundreds of restaurants in China, in 2008 opening its 1,000th location in Dongguan, Guangdong. Existing locations in the USA were refurbished as well.

Skinner also remained open to ideas for new products. In 2009, for example, McDonald's launched McCafe in its US restaurants – selling a range of lattes, cappuccinos and mochas – in order to compete against such coffee companies as Starbucks. In 2010, further encouraging its new 'cafe culture', it offered free Wi-Fi Internet at 11,000 of its restaurants. "If we can find goods and services or a product or technology that we could leverage through 31,000 [locations], that would be the only thing we would consider," Skinner said.

This is similar to the approach Ray Kroc took five decades earlier when McDonald's was still a fledgling business getting off the ground. His commitment to quality, cleanliness and unsurpassed customer service laid the groundwork for what has become the largest fast-food franchise in the world. Those basic business tenets are what will carry the company through the next 50 years.

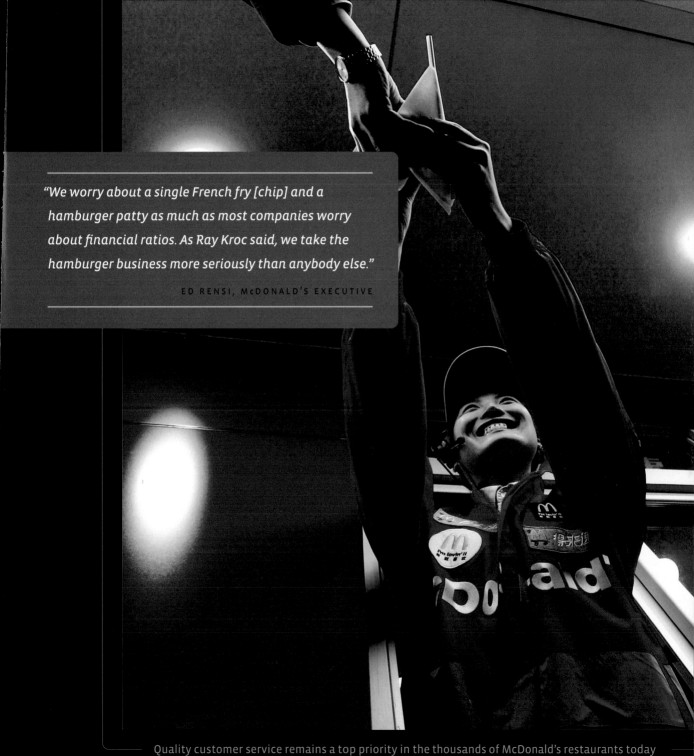

"We worry about a single French fry [chip] and a hamburger patty as much as most companies worry about financial ratios. As Ray Kroc said, we take the hamburger business more seriously than anybody else."

ED RENSI, McDONALD'S EXECUTIVE

Quality customer service remains a top priority in the thousands of McDonald's restaurants today

THE FACE OF THE FRANCHISE

Almost every child in America knows Ronald McDonald. In fact, according to the 2001 book *Fast Food Nation*, only Father Christmas is more recognisable to schoolchildren than McDonald's red-haired clown. His yellow jumpsuit and floppy red shoes have been associated with the restaurant from 1963 when Willard Scott (who later became better known as the weatherman for the *Today* show on US television) first appeared with a paper cup attached to his nose and a fast-food tray propped on his head in local McDonald's adverts in Washington, DC. By 1965, Ronald had become the cornerstone of the franchise's advertising campaigns and Scott had been replaced by a younger, trimmer actor. While Ronald's costume has evolved over the years, his appearance – from the red wig and nose to the ballooning yellow suit and striped socks – has now become part of the corporate identity. The clown even has an official title: Chief Happiness Officer.

GLOSSARY

acquisitions the purchase of companies by other companies

board of directors a group of people in charge of making big decisions for a publicly owned company

brand the name of a product or manufacturer; a brand distinguishes a product from similar products made by other manufacturers

brokers individuals or firms that act as mediators between a buyer and seller, usually charging a fee for those services

cash flow the amounts of money received and spent by a company

conglomerates corporations consisting of several companies in different businesses

debt the condition of owing something to another person or entity

executive a decision-making leader of a company such as the president or chief executive officer (CEO)

fast food inexpensive food such as hamburgers, chips and fried chicken which is prepared and served quickly

franchise to extend a successful product or service to other businesses (called franchisees) which operate under the franchisor's trade name in exchange for a fee and often a portion of the profits

initial public offering the first sale of stock by a company to the public; this is generally done to raise funds for the company, which is then owned by investors rather than an individual or group of individuals

jingles catchy, often musical slogans used in advertising campaigns

lease a written agreement under which a property owner allows a tenant to use the property for a specified period of time and rent

lenders people or institutions such as banks which provide money to another person or business temporarily

market share the percentage of the total sales of a given type of product or service that is attributable to a particular company

marketing advertising and promoting a product in order to increase sales

net income the total income a company has after subtracting costs and expenses from the money it makes

revenue the money earned by a company; another word for income

sponsor a person or organisation that finances a project or event carried out by another person or group, often as a means of advertising

1955 First McDonald's restaurant opens in Des Plaines, Illinois

1960 A total of 200 franchises operate in 12 US states

1963 One billionth McDonald's hamburger is sold

1965 McDonald's becomes a publicly owned company; shares boost the company's finances

1967 McDonald's sponsors the Super Bowl; Big Mac introduced

1970 Five billionth McDonald's hamburger sold

1983 Chicken McNuggets introduced; becomes a huge success

1988 Over 10,000 McDonald's restaurants trade globally

1990–1992 McDonald's opens shops in Moscow and Beijing

2002 McDonald's shuts down 200 US locations and redundancies are made for first time ever

2004 Film *Super Size Me* dents confidence in McDonald's menu

2005 A bold, futuristic McDonald's branch opens in Chicago commemorating the company's 50th anniversary

2006 McDonald's share price rises by 25 per cent

2009 McCafe installed in all US premises selling coffee drinks

2010 Free Wi-Fi Internet offered at 11,000 McDonald's locations

INDEX

A

advertising 14, 16, 18, 42, 45
   television adverts 14, 16, 18
      Super Bowl (1966) 16, 18
Arch Deluxe 34
Arend, Rene 26

B

Beijing, China 32
Big Mac 18, 21, 34, 37
Boston Market 38, 40
Burger Chef 22
Burger King 22, 34

C

Canada 24
Cantalupo, Jim 40, 42
Chicago, Illinois 5, 6, 8, 17, 24
Chicken McNuggets 26
China 42
Chipotle Mexican Grill 38, 40
Crispy Chicken Deluxe 34

D

Delligatti, Jim 21
Des Plaines, Illinois 5, 8, 42

E

Egg McMuffin 26, 37
Europe 24

F

Filet-O-Fish sandwich 18
Fish Filet Deluxe 34
Franchise Realty Corporation 10

G

Golden Arches 5, 13, 16
Greenberg, Jack 34, 38, 40
Grilled Chicken Deluxe 34

H

Happy Meals 26, 37
Hulaburger 18

I

Israel 32

J

Jack in the Box 22

K

Kentucky Fried Chicken 26
Kroc, Ray 6, 8, 10, 14, 16, 18, 24, 26, 29, 30, 35, 42

M

Martino, June 16
McDonald, Dick 6, 8, 10, 13, 14
McDonald, Mac 6, 8, 10, 13, 14
McDonald's Corporation
   employee redundancies 38, 40
   first franchisee restaurant 5, 8, 42
   international business 24
   menu 18, 21, 26, 32, 34, 40, 42
      fat content controversy 32, 37, 40
   original restaurant 6, 13, 29
   recyclable products 32, 34
   revenue 8, 10, 24, 26, 30, 38
McDonald's System, Inc. 8
McLean Deluxe 32
Meston, Stanley 13
Minnie Pearl's Chicken 22
Moscow, Russia 30, 32
multi-mixer machines 6, 8, 29

O

Oak Brook, Illinois 8

P

Poland 32
Puerto Rico 24

Q

Quinlan, Michael 30, 34

R

Ronald McDonald 14, 34, 45

S

San Bernardino, California 6, 29
Scott, Willard 45
Shamrock Shake 18
Skinner, Jim 42
Sonneborn, Harry 10, 16, 18, 22
Speedee Service System 6
stock 16, 40, 42
Super Size Me 40

T

Turner, Fred 8, 18, 22, 24, 26, 30, 40

W

Waukegan, Illinois 8
Wendy's 22, 34